Customer-Driven Budgeting

Customer-Driven Budgeting

Prepare, Engage, Execute:
The Small Business Guide
for Growth

Floyd Talbot

Customer-Driven Budgeting: Prepare, Engage, Execute: The Small Business Guide for Growth

First published in 2012 by
Business Expert Press, LLC
222 East 46th Street, New York, NY 10017
www.businessexpertpress.com

ISBN-13: 978-1-60649-429-5 (paperback)

ISBN-13: 978-1-60649-430-1 (e-book)

DOI: 10.4128/9781606494301

Business Expert Press Managerial Accounting collection

Collection ISSN: 2152-7113 (print)
Collection ISSN: 2152-7121 (electronic)

Cover design by Jonathan Pennell
Interior design by Exeter Premedia Services Private Ltd., Chennai, India

First edition: 2012

10 9 8 7 6 5 4 3 2 1

Printed in the United States of America.

Abstract

This comprehensive budgeting book emphasizes that the customer drives the business organization and processes and becomes the overriding purpose for a company's existence and success. *Customer-Driven Budgeting* offers a complete guide that covers every step in the budgeting cycle from the basics of organization, processes, and funding to budget execution and monitoring. It emphasizes that the budget is the starting point and catalyst for gaining customers. The budget prepares the company to supply the sales and marketing team reinforcements for giving a compelling reason for customers to buy from it.

The customer is the object of every effort and dollar and drives the business, its goals, practices, processes, and activities. The market-focused, customer-driven principle takes budgeting out of the finance organization and pushes it into production, shipping and receiving, purchasing, inventory management, IT, and outside the doors to vendors, bankers, investors, and others business partners. This book explains the treatment of these constituents in the budget. This book is one that can be used immediately in business budgeting. Its modular format permits the reader to start at the beginning of the budget process and work through it entirely or select a budget area most challenging to the business and work from there to other areas of priority. Given that this book covers the entire budget process, the author recommends following the format as presented to coalesce around the budget team.

Keywords

budgeting, budget, financial management, strategy, customer, small business, small business owner, cash flow, investors, business management, growth, objectives, performance, measurements, processes, manage, management, financial statements, pro forma financial statements, best practices, customer management, vendor management, organization, capital budget, benchmarks, benchmarking, financial ratios, staffing, production planning, outsourcing, outsource, risk management, risks, revenue, accounting, planning, metrics, evaluation, financial performance, sales, marketing, markets, vendors

Contents

List of Figures

List of Tables

Acknowledgments

This book could not come to fruition without several key individuals in support of it. Foremost in this effort is my wife, Vickie, who gave her time, support, and dedication to reviewing the manuscript and recommending changes. It took two very important disciplines for this book: writing and business management. Two key professors helped me refine my writing skills with their red pens: Dr. Gary Tuck and Dr. James Sawyer. Much thanks to professional colleagues and fellow Pepperdine University Graziadio School of Business and Management alumni Chris Mackey, Director of Business Development at CPP, Inc. and Sergio Retamal, President and CEO of Global4PL Supply Chain Services. Thanks, also, to Tim Frame, CPA and Partner of Walton & Frame and Ed Correia, CEO of Sagacent Technologies, Inc., whose business was a winner of the 2012 SMB Top 150 Award. In addition, I thank the editorial and production staff at Business Expert Press for all the hard work each person contributed.

Read First!

The Audience for this Book

This book concerns customer-driven budgeting. That is, companies in which customers rank as top priority who will profit from this book's contents. This book is for any small business owner, President, CEO, CFO, board member, or investor who wants to realize success for their business or portfolio investment. From the start-up firm to the $25–$50 million corporations confronting the challenges of financial and business management, this book will provide a wealth of value and information. Is your business in start-up mode with its first or second round of funding? You will find the budgeting principles in this book useful for exercising sound financial management. The critical timeframe for start-up businesses is the first five years. During this time, businesses are more prone to bankruptcy or simply going out of business. Companies during this period need sound financial and cash flow management. Companies in business for more than five years seeking to increase market penetration, profits, and greater value for the owners and shareholders will find the principles and practices outlined in this book valuable for putting in place sound forecasting practices. This book provides an essential roadmap of best practices for aiding financial institutions, angel investors, and venture capitalists in helping their portfolio companies to succeed.

The Practice of Budgeting

This book arises out of the good, bad, and ugly of business management and practices. The good taught me successful practices, while the bad and ugly led to wisdom. Over the tenure of my career in business and financial management, I observed many companies fold or suffer financially. They failed to implement sound financial management practices, especially the practice of budgeting. I also made my share of mistakes in business practices and grew through them. One of the more important things I learned is that money management is a top priority. A sage once said: you rarely make right decisions; rather you make decisions and then make them right. That is what business practices are all about. You practice through successes and pitfalls, refining your decision-making until right decisions far outweigh the wrong ones.

Business owners and executives do not make right decisions all the time. Otherwise, business failures would cease to exist. Statistics concerning business failures illustrate that right decisions do not constitute the norm. About 60% of start-up businesses fail within the first five years. That amounts to a lot of mistakes and decision-making gone awry. The practice of planning, of which budgeting is a major component, shares a top spot on the list.

Making decisions right *is* the norm. We are not prophets and know what the future throws at us. Everyone makes mistakes that cast them and their business temporarily off course because the future throws curves. Making decisions right is the course correction from lessons learned. Sound business practices, especially budgeting is no exception. We learn by doing, discovering, and repeating. The good, bad, and ugly bring best practices to fruition.

This book aims at success for you and your company. A corollary to this success is the design and implementation of best practices foundational to it and management direction. This book represents a process template for business budgeting. As a template, you can overlay it on your existing budgeting cycle, adding what segments you may need to fill in the missing gaps. If your company is new to budgeting, this template will guide you through the entire budget cycle from start to finish (see Chapters 2 and 3 about the budget cycle and scheduling).

The budget process does not end when you finalize your budget. Rather, the final budget is just the beginning of the budget cycle. Its conclusion arrives at the completion of the budgeted period. The major portion of the budget cycle commences after you finalize the budget and move into the fiscal period the budget covers. This begins the real work of the budget cycle: transactional analysis, reviews, financial reporting, corrective actions, performance evaluations, lessons learned, and preparation for the next cycle. Management and decision-making summarize this tough work.

The budget is one of the primary best practices you can have for managing your business. Budgeting is a problem-solver for your business. This book address 10 challenging problems businesses frequently encounter that throw up roadblocks to success and could lead to failure and bankruptcy (see Chapter 1). When addressing these challenges, budgeting acts as their painkiller.

Budgets set targets, managerial controls, accountability, responsibility, and benchmarks. This book will address these practice issues in their respective chapters. In essence, this book is primarily about management. Managing consists of more than numbers, tracking transactions, maximizing profits, paying taxes, and keeping the Internal Revenue Service (IRS), competition, and the regulatory authorities at bay. Rather, managing the business is managing an organization and its constituents so that they can support you in reaching your goals, growing your business, and maximizing value and wealth (see Chapters 5–7).

Customers make up your primary constituent. Customer requirements pave the roadmap for yours and their success. Nothing rates higher in the business than the customer. Peter Drucker asked a very simple question that sometimes has an elusive and not readily forthcoming answer: "Who is the customer?" He writes,

> "Who is the customer?" is the first and crucial question in defining business purpose and business mission. It is not an easy, let alone an obvious question. How it is being answered determines, in large measure, how the business defines itself.[1]

If the guru of modern management considered the question not at all obvious and the answer equally so, can it be that a large number of entrepreneurs have similar challenges with it? That is the reason why this book has "customer" in its title.

Budgeting and Management

Managing your business is also about managing segments or components of your business. Your business cannot survive and move toward its mission and goals without sound management principles for guiding and winning your constituents. While this is so, this book is not a tome on management but rather is about practicing certain principles of management. For creating a sharper focus on your customer and other constituents lending to your success, this book introduces the concept of Key Management Areas (KMAs). Chapter 7 delves more into the explanation of KMAs.

KMAs identify the managerial segments of your business that align with your constituents and comprise the managerial chart. KMAs are the components in which activity occurs, hand-offs between one area of the business and another transpire, and management controls exist for better management of the organization, processes, and funding for sales and operations. That is the reason this book identifies them as management areas. This is where management happens. This book addresses not only management and constituents but also the essentials of processes and their importance in preparing a comprehensive budget.

Figure 1 illustrates the budget template as a managerial tool. The budget provides *management direction* by

1. setting objectives;
2. preparing performance criteria;
3. calling for accountability;
4. creating measurements.

The budget offers *constituent management* in that it considers and treats each constituent as a business partner that provides a source of business success. The budget makes the primary constituent, the customer, the business driver. It integrates and orients all other constituents toward customer cultivation, satisfaction, and retention through the mission statement, objectives, and planning activities. The budget serves as the *business problem-solver* in that it is solutions based and applies those solutions to the challenges and pain points it encounters toward meeting stated objectives in the marketplace. The budget provides *business*

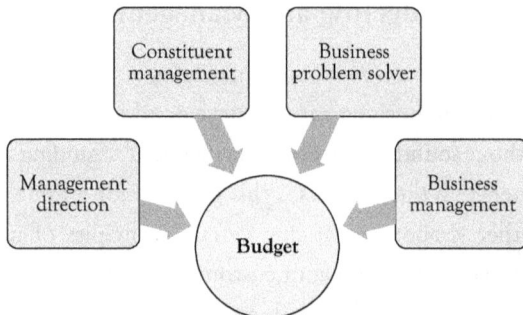

Figure 1. The managerial and solutions basis of budgeting.

management by becoming the financial management practice, discipline, driver, and focus for the entire organization and its processes. It is the business management roadmap and measurement of success (see Stage II, *The Pro Forma Financial Statements*).

Key Managerial Practices

As you work your way through the chapters, you will notice that they build the budget on fundamental business practices. For this reason, this book emphasizes a review of organizations and processes for incorporating budget funding for improvements. The budget is not simply a numbers assignment for revenue and resources. Consequently, the budget considers Kaizen, that is, continuous improvement toward increased business value.[2] Kaizen is Japanese term for "improvement." The Kaizen movement arose from the work of William Edwards Deming's consultation with companies in Japan beginning in the 1950s. While this book is not about Kaizen, it focuses on certain practices it considers essential for successful enterprises in any industry or company.

One of the most fundamental focuses for business success emphasized in this book is process. In fact, this book raises one process as a primary priority—the process of budgeting. Chapter 6 discusses the process of budgeting and the importance of reviewing processes in a company as a preliminary step of budgeting. The reason for dedication to processes for the budget is threefold:

1. Processes require resources—human, material, and capital.
2. Processes drive the organization and business toward its mission.
3. Processes touch upon core areas of business success:
   a. The control environment
   b. Risk management
   c. Activities and transactions
   d. Reporting
   e. Monitoring and review.

Monitoring and review is really a primary key for continuous improvement and follows the path of the budget cycle during the budget execution phase and financial reviews (Chapters 14 and 15) toward the beginning of the next fiscal period.

The *Business Budget Builder*: A Resource to Get Started

The Microsoft Excel workbook called *Business Budget Builder* is available as a download from the publisher's website. Its purpose is to provide users with a tool for doing any one of the following:

1. Creating a comprehensive budget resulting in a full set of pro forma financial statements and measurements for them
2. Using any one of the included spreadsheets in a standalone manner to identify specific costs or expenses, such as total payroll, gross margin, or capital budget
3. Identifying a comprehensive sales and marketing expense plan
4. Creating a capital budget and identifying return on investment of capital outlays

The purchase of the book, *Customer-driven Budgeting: Prepare, Engage, Execute: The Small Business Guide for Growth*, grants you the use of this Excel workbook application for your entire company for preparing your budget in conjunction with this book.

Excel Application Warranty Disclaimer and Software Application License Agreement

PLEASE READ THE BELOW SECTION CAREFULLY. IT INCLUDES WARRANTY INFORMATION AND A LICENSE AGREEMENT APPLICABLE TO THE USE OF THE DOWNLOADABLE MICROSOFT EXCEL SOFTWARE APPLICATION REFERRED TO AS *BUSINESS BUDGET BUILDER*.

Warranty Disclaimer

The Microsoft Excel software application called *Business Budget Builder* is made available only to purchasers of the book *Customer-driven*

Budgeting: Prepare, Engage, Execute: The Small Business Guide for Growth. Use of this application by those other than those purchasing the book is not permitted under copyright law or this license.

This Microsoft Excel workbook comes with no warranties, conditions, representations, or terms concerning matters of performance, results, merchantability, integration, quality, or fitness for any purpose whether expressed or implied. The author makes no representations about the suitability of the content, format, or functionality as it applies to the expectations of the user(s). While the author made every effort to create an Excel application that renders accurate results from the entries users make to it, the author or publisher cannot be liable for results that do not meet the users' expectations due to made entries or modifications to the application's formatting or functionality. While the author makes this disclaimer, he also regards that this Microsoft Excel application can prove to be useful with its numerous features and functions for leading to a successful budget plan.

Software Application License Agreement

If you have obtained the software application from the publisher or author along with the book, *Customer-driven Budgeting*, the publisher and author grants a single license for its use according to the following limitations.

Use

You may use the Microsoft Excel *Business Budget Builder* application on only one computer or place it on a server or your network to be shared with designated users as specified under the Share Workbook function. The Microsoft Excel workbook application cannot be installed on multiple computers under this license. Doing so may also prevent the use of its intended purpose of being a multiuser application. This application also may not be licensed or distributed to others who did not purchase the book. Additionally, this application may not be renamed and used under a different name. You may make a backup copy of this Excel application under the condition that the backup will not be used on other computers or be renamed for use by the business or individual purchasing the corresponding book.

Modification

Copyright and licensing of the *Business Budget Builder* prevents modification or the derivation of its design or functions for use in or with other developed Excel applications without expressed written permission of the author. Doing so could prevent the *Business Budget Builder* from functioning according to its intended purpose.

Optimizing Your Budget Process

To optimize your budget process, the author advises that you make use of all available tools and resources for preparing your budget and sound financial management. Take advantage of any features or functionalities within your accounting system and other software applications for increasing efficiency for your financial forecast.

If you do not have budget development tools or tools to generate the numbers for your pro forma financial statements, the spreadsheets in this workbook will provide you a great start. The *Business Budget Builder* has a menu to guide you through the entire workbook. As you work through the menu items, you will be able to develop the following for your budget:

1. A menu-driven means for working through and completing a comprehensive budget for your business
2. A fully developed project task list for completing your budget
3. A mechanism for making certain budget assumptions or parameters that automatically produce specific budget forecasts
4. A sales and marketing plan from the bottom up that considers not only existing products but also new product introductions for giving you the confidence that you have left nothing to chance
5. A means of spreading sales revenue according to seasonal factors (e.g., a retail company)
6. An expansion "what if" scenario that other budget plans do not consider that provides for assumptions for expansion into new channels, new locations and markets, and mergers and acquisitions

7. A capital budget plan that considers all capital outlays and provides you with the means of determining the most cost-efficient approach

8. A comprehensive staffing plan that considers not only headcount and hire date but also taxes and other burden costs with a top level summary

9. A 12-month operating plan and a set of all three pro forma financial statements

10. A financial performance execution plan with a set of financial ratio measurements for keeping you focused on performance

While you can use any of the individual spreadsheets in a standalone fashion, in doing so you will soon discover the entire workbook becomes a highly useful tool for preparing a comprehensive budget.

Instructions for the Microsoft Excel Workbook

TO THE PURCHASER OF *CUSTOMER-DRIVEN BUDGETING*: Along with this book, your purchase includes one licensed copy of the Microsoft Excel workbook *Business Budget Builder* as described above. Make sure that you also download the instructions manual for operating the *Business Budget Builder* in multiuser access mode. The title of this instructions manual is *Using the Business Budget Builder Excel Workbook in Multi-user Access Mode*.

Each spreadsheet comes with its own set of instructions. Before you begin, hover on the cell that brings up the instructions for that spreadsheet. In addition, each chapter refers to the *Business Budget Builder* Microsoft Excel workbook if it applies. As you read the respective chapters, you will notice illustrations that show segments of the relevant spreadsheet(s) to each chapter. When you complete the *Business Budget Builder* workbook, you will have a complete set of pro forma financial statements and a monthly operating income statement for your budget year. One or more spreadsheets in the workbook correspond to the respective chapters. Table 1 provides an index to the Microsoft Excel workbook spreadsheets.

Table 1. Index to the Business Budget Builder Microsoft Excel Workbook

Customer-driven Budgeting and the Business Budget Builder Microsoft Excel Workbook Index	
Book Chapter	**Microsoft Excel workbook spreadsheet**
—	Set up List, Parameters Setup
Chapter Two The Budget Cycle	Management Team
Chapter Three Budget Schedule	Budget Project Schedule
Chapter Four Objectives, Performance, and Measurements	—
Chapter Five Organizational Review	—
Chapter Six Processes Review	—
Chapter Seven Key Management Areas	—
Chapter Eight Sales Plan	Product List, Sales Detail, Sales and Marketing, Market Expansion, Headcount
Chapter Nine Capital Plan	Capital Budget, Capital Equipment Evaluation
Chapter Ten Production Plan	Inventory Budget, Headcount, Research and Development
Chapter Eleven Administrative Plan	Headcount, Payroll Summary
Chapter Twelve Total Staffing Plan	Headcount, Payroll Summary
Chapter Thirteen Pro Forma Financial Statements	Operating Budget, Cash Flow, Pro forma Financial Statements, Financial Ratios
Chapter Fourteen Execution Plan	Financial Ratios
Chapter Fifteen Period Ending Financial Reviews	Financial Ratios

STAGE I

Budget Pre-planning

I prefer essentials and options, but my budget sometimes cannot afford both.

CHAPTER 1

Before You Begin

Everything has a beginning; you must start somewhere, so start intentionally.

Organization of the Book

This book has three parts:

1. Preplanning steps for preparing the company for the budgeting process
2. Preparing the budget: pro forma financial statements and business measurements
3. Implementation and ongoing monitoring for meeting stated objectives

Each step supports the next and builds on the previous one toward success in gaining and retaining customers. The first step lays the groundwork. The second builds upon it with an informed forecast. The third tracks and measures business performance for planning and determining success in meeting set objectives and business mission.

Budgeting, Beyond Budgeting, or No Budget

Why budget at all? A number of business leaders and professionals take the approach that the budget is a relic of the past and needs elimination. They say forget the budget and focus more on controlling the bottom line. As early as 2003, Jeremy Hope and Robin Fraser called for its abolishment, associating it with "centralized hierarchies" and that it concentrates on the minutia of telephone bills or entertainment allowances.[1] Hope and Fraser advocated the concept of beyond budgeting as an "adaptive performance management" approach to budget that arose from dissatisfaction with the traditional approaches.

It has many pluses but appears lacking in attention to a comprehensive approach to financial management that includes targeting, management controls, risks evaluation, discipline, and best practices assessment. In fact, the budget does lead to controlling the bottom line, especially within the context of a team effort whose decisions drive the business. Hope and Fraser's dissatisfaction with the traditional approaches appear to arise from frustrations with a heavy-handed executive approach and perhaps hidden agendas from chief executive officers (CEOs) and chief financial officers (CFOs) rather than providing empowerment at all management levels.[2]

While pronouncing corporate budgeting as a "joke" that turns "business decisions into elaborate exercises" and promotes cheating, Michael Jenson notes that the budget process is not the root cause.[3] However, discarding a practice due to dishonesty does not solve financial management challenges. In fact, it may be disruptive in giving the real problems a pass while casting aside the benefits of sound practices implemented effectively. In the case with Hope, Fraser, and Jensen, the core issue was not the budget process itself but other variables integrated into the practice that placed hindrances in the way and disrupting the process. While the *beyond budgeting* or "discard the budget" factions bring valuable benefits to the financial management table, they appear not to address the ancillary issues that may be hindering budget practices such as hidden agendas or deceit. This book advocates assuming the benefits of budgeting, while integrating the best of other practices. Budgeting aids in solving a number of challenges that businesses encounter.

Ten Business Challenges Solved Through Budgeting

Budgeting provides a precrisis and crisis preventive solution. It solves a number of challenges that hinder market reach and growth. Without budgeting, organizations can be caught off guard with a lack of direction and measurements for growth. Among the challenges budgeting resolves are the following:

1. *The challenge of customer cultivation.* The intensity of competition in the marketplace gives customers options. The budget process provides the environment for creating a "so what?" message that supplies the sales and marketing organizations reinforcements for giving a compelling reason for customers to buy and stay with a company. The "so what" message is the differentiator that arises from collaborative efforts, during the budget process. By placing customers in the center of the budget process, the company will not take them for granted and will be prepared to reply with cogent messages when customers say, "So what, your competitors have that too."

2. *The challenge of narrow or negative profits.* The mystery of a disappearing bottom line can leave management stunned. "What happened?" is a common phrase. The budget complements the business plan through reachable and realistic targets for revenues, expenses, and profits.

3. *The challenge of surprising tax liabilities.* The budget provides a plan for managing tax liabilities and the potential for tax reduction. The budget plan anticipates such tax liabilities. Tim Frame of Walton and Frame Certified Public Accountants recommends laying the groundwork in the budget by collaborating your company's CPA firm for developing "a set of worksheets to be used by the CFO or Treasurer in order to develop and record a monthly or quarterly provision for income taxes."[4] This groundwork minimizes surprises and keeps your business abreast of tax law and liabilities.

4. *The challenge of money management.* Often, budgeting focuses on the organizational chart rather than a managerial chart. This book highlights the concept of Key Management Areas (KMAs). KMAs are the critical components of the company common to all businesses but given secondary priority by most. Readers will identify KMAs for allocating and managing resources, processes, and funds toward product delivery and customer satisfaction.

5. *The challenge of theft, embezzlement, and fraud.* These events cost businesses millions of dollars annually. One of the most often neglected budgetary items is that of allocating funding for the best practice internal controls for safeguarding the business. The budget

plans and allocates funds for implementing safeguards to close gaps leading to losses.

6. *The challenge of planning discipline.* Budgeting is a planning practice that instills financial discipline in the organization. It reduces firefighting, tension, a hurried and haphazard execution, and the omission of important activities for organized and successful business and financial management. Effective and successful companies need discipline.

7. *The challenge of setting priorities.* Budgeting determines mutually recognized and accepted priorities and aids in reducing or eliminating activities and costs not contributing to those priorities.

8. *The challenge of company-wide communications and expectations concerning mission, objectives, and results.* The budget not only provides clear direction for financial targets but also aids in building a cohesive team for bringing about desired results through that cohesiveness.

9. *The challenge of the market.* The market can be volatile and unpredictable. However, budgeting brings market focus for funds to reach it and through the process enables the budget team to crystallize a plan for addressing the market and competition.

10. *The challenge of performance measurement and business and financial execution.* The budget not only creates a foundation for financial and business management but also provides the framework for performance measurement and budget execution, addressing key challenges, identifying lessons learned, and taking corrective action.

Budgeting and Other Planning Methodologies

Preparation and a sound execution plan provide the strength of budgeting. A missing execution plan diminishes the power of the budget in leading the business toward success. Budgets normally cover a full year with possible forecasts beyond one year on a quarterly basis to recognize the revenue or costs of specific objectives that overlap budget periods. These planned quarterly forecasts are important because they assume that certain objectives may encompass more than one fiscal year and markets and the economy change. Showing the full extent of expenses and revenues from an objective is useful for financial impact of objective completion. In addition, forecasts and re-forecasts keep your business current with the volatility of markets and the economy. They provide means of readdressing budget assumptions, objectives, opportunity, and negative impact.

Budgeting and Strategic Planning

The strategic and business plans carry business forecasts and targets beyond the budgeted year to 3–5 years. The budget normally encompasses 1 year, so there are several budgeted periods associated with a strategic plan. The budget is the place where the firm identifies the baseline for the budget and integrates the strategies with that baseline. The baseline consists of the revenues, expenses, and applied capital that the company would realize before objective setting or strategic planning. To account for the revenues and costs to realize the objectives from the strategic plan, you should also reflect these objectives in the budget. Figure 1.1 illustrates the relationships between the financial baseline, strategic plan, and budget.

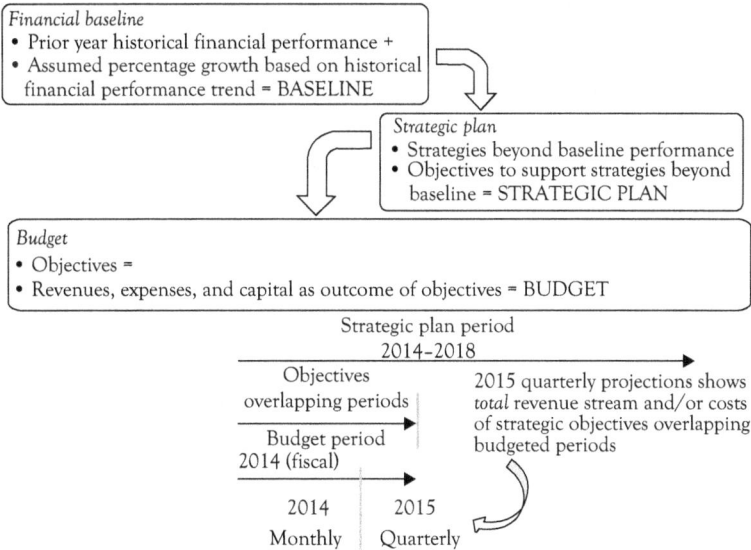

Financial baseline
- Prior year historical financial performance +
- Assumed percentage growth based on historical financial performance trend = BASELINE

Strategic plan
- Strategies beyond baseline performance
- Objectives to support strategies beyond baseline = STRATEGIC PLAN

Budget
- Objectives =
- Revenues, expenses, and capital as outcome of objectives = BUDGET

Strategic plan period
2014–2018

Objectives overlapping periods

2015 quarterly projections shows *total* revenue stream and/or costs of strategic objectives overlapping budgeted periods

Budget period 2014 (fiscal)

| 2014 | 2015 |
| Monthly | Quarterly |

Figure 1.1. Relation between the financial baseline, strategic plan, and the budget.

The Customer as the Driver of Budgeting

In addition to goals, for a large number of companies the customer drives business organizational and processes management. For these companies, the customer becomes the overriding purpose for its existence and success. From the outset, the business integrates the customer focus into the budgeting cycle from the basics of organization, processes, and funding to budget execution and monitoring. The budget is the starting point and catalyst for focusing on customers. The budget prepares the company to supply the sales and marketing team reinforcements for giving a compelling reason for customers to buy.

The customer-driven principle takes budgeting out of the finance organization and pushes it into production, shipping and receiving, purchasing, inventory management, IT, and outside the doors to vendors, bankers, investors, and other business partners. This book explains the treatment of these partners in the budget, especially the customer. It reveals how the company harnesses the strength of its partners for making them and the company successful.

The budget process provides the opportunity to focus on the customer at each step. The budget spells out the goals, activities, and funds for its implementation. When a company places itself in its customer's shoes, it gets a very different perspective. This perspective drives the budget process, its goals, and activities.

The budget process is the driving force that runs through the organization, its processes, and the money that funds both of them. Figure 1.2

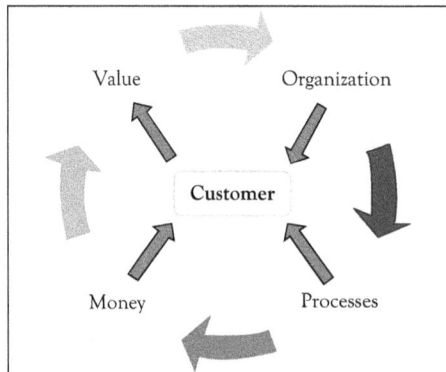

Figure 1.2. Customer-driven business value.

illustrates how the customer drives business value. It shows the connection between strengthening the three business building blocks and their focus on how the customer increases company value. The customer in turn contributes to business value. During the course of the budget process, the customer has a place on the agenda when discussing organizational and process improvements and funding requirements. Chapter 2 discusses a proposed agenda for the budget process.

Action Items for the Budget Team

Consider starting a checklist on any of the 10 challenges discussed in this chapter as a beginning step, prior to the budgeting process. This will help you identify objectives related to them for your budget team and their corresponding costs for incorporation into the budget.

1. The challenge of customer cultivation: Prepare a strengths and weaknesses statement for customer relationship management. Consider criteria such as
   a. follow up;
   b. warranty service time;
   c. communications on updates, new services, and satisfaction;
   d. technical support;
   e. staying in touch;
   f. customer satisfaction; and
   g. customer loyalty to the brand.

   As part of your budget cycle, you may wish to investigate methodologies for benchmarking your customer relations. Jean Creech Avent prepared an excellent background paper on *Customer Relationship Index* that can be helpful in developing a benchmark for strengthening your company's customer relationships. He discusses the relationship between a given customer relationship score and financial performance indicators. He also focuses on how the index distinguishes between customer relationship leaders and those who are not leaders.[5]
2. The challenge of narrow or negative profits: Review financial trends for the past 2–3 years, specifically monthly trends for the most

current fiscal year. What do they reveal regarding your revenues and expenses? Which expenses stand out that may be the cause for concern? Do you see volatile fluctuations or spikes in revenues or expenses? Why are there revenue spikes? Are there one-time customers? Are there large single-customer purchases that may not repeat?

3. The challenge of surprising tax liabilities: What did a review of your tax liabilities for prior years reveal? Do specific issues stand out? Do you make quarterly tax payments? Can you identify any necessary corrective actions from your observations for reducing tax liabilities?

4. The challenge of financial management: Financial management incorporates discipline, priority, and direction, according to set targets. Review your current financial management processes for identifying weaknesses and gaps in required financial data for strategic decision-making.

5. The challenge of theft, embezzlement, fraud, and other losses: The budget cycle is the place to consider where you may have safeguard exposures. Ensure that this item is high on the agenda for your budget kick-off meeting.

6. Once the budget team recognizes that you have placed the budget process as a high priority, the challenge of setting priorities is softened. Your focus on company priorities also communicates your expectations to your staff. During this preplanning stage, it is a good idea to focus your staff on the company mission so that they understand that the budget process is an integrated part of that mission.

7. Part of expectations consists of performance measurements. Ensure that your team is performance measurement oriented. This sets their expectations that their performance individually and as a team influences their success as well as the company's success. Chapter 5 discusses the levels of performance and their measurements.

Saving Budget Practice Records and Systems

Budgeting is a continuing practice that once documented provides a valuable system for each budget year. For this reason, your company will benefit the most from archiving all the documentation from your budget activities. You can set up a collaborative environment on your network.

Such a collaborative environment allows you to maintain all documentation in one place with easy budget team access at any time. In addition, rather than reinventing the budget wheel in the next budget cycle, you can retrieve what you did the previous year. This access and retrieval capability permits you to establish your budget baseline for subsequent budget cycles.

CHAPTER 2

Budget Cycle

Without action, inertia and stagnation create rigor mortis in the business.

Objectives

After completing this chapter, you will be able to accomplish the following toward the budget process:

1. Identify the components of a well-development budget for execution
2. Set the foundation for the entire budget cycle through the budget vision, leadership, and the agenda
3. Be able to complete the Management Team spreadsheet in the optional *Business Budget Builder* Microsoft Excel workbook that accompanies this book

Preplanning Activities

Four premises of this book are as follows:

1. The bases of budgeting are flexibility and adapting to the economy, market, and challenges the company encounters after completing the initial budget.
2. The budget quantifies the business or strategic plan.
3. The budget is a routine business practice along with other routine tasks and projects in the company.
4. The budget is a collaborative effort with segment owners for fulfilling the company's mission and objectives.

A number of activities occur before beginning the budget process for a successful and timely implementation. These activities are no more than what you would normally undertake when planning daily, weekly, or monthly. The only difference is that the timeframe is longer and scope larger. Consequently, budgeting does not have to be an added event to an already crowded business calendar. Rather, like all other planned business events, it should be an integrated practice of your business like all other business practices. Treating it as such contributes to greater success in execution.

Budget activity is unceasing. Consequently, the entire budgeting team must champion this concept to be cohesive in the budgeting approach and for total business management. Successful business decisions depend on those who champion practices that lend to accomplishing business growth goals. Unless the team sees goals through the lens of the practice of budgeting, the prospect of a successful future diminishes in proportion to its inattention.

This book suggests the following budgeting steps:

1. Roles and responsibilities
2. The budget project schedule
3. Kick-off meeting, agenda, and preplanning tasks
4. Sales plan
5. Capital plan
6. Production plan
7. Administrative plan
8. Total staffing plan
9. Budgeted pro forma financial statements
10. Execution plan and ongoing performance reviews

Budget Team's Roles and Responsibilities

The budget process begins with people. A team prepares a budget to allocate resources for executing business performance. People are the decision drivers in the business. People manage other people who manage people, capital, and materials toward production of products and services for customer requirements. People are the thinking behind results. Peter Drucker wrote, "People decisions are the ultimate—perhaps the only—control of the organization. People determine the performance capacity of an organization. No organization can do better than the people it has."[1] His statement is basic but profound with a wide range of applications.

Defining management roles and responsibilities is the first step toward the budgeting process. Identifying team managers and their roles on the team insures budget preparation and execution success. Each team member is an entrepreneur who owns a portion of the business and manages it toward the company's success. It takes teamwork to ensure that the entire organization supports the budget.

The Budget Kick-off Meeting and Agenda

The kick-off meeting is perhaps the most important meeting in preplanning and the entire budget cycle. It sets the stage for the total project and thereby must take high priority by all participants, especially the budget leader.

Before the Kick-off Meeting

The budget process consists of several preplanning activities. The most important items consist of

1. ensuring that all participants are prepared to commit to the project;
2. setting a date and time for a kick-off meeting;
3. preparing the budget agenda to be sent to all participants prior to the kick-off meeting;
4. assigning action items to be completed prior to the meeting; and
5. emphasizing the importance of everyone's participation.

If your organization is new to budgeting, be aware that those on the budget team may not view the budget process as an integrated activity among all other operational activities. To most, the budget is an annual event added to current operational activities and transactions. If this is the case, the kick-off meeting is the place to discuss the role of budgeting as an event that continues throughout the fiscal year. It is a process like all others in the business equal to other business practices. The budget process does not stop when the team completes it. Rather its execution lasts the entire year. This principle sets expectations for team managers.

The Budget Kick-off Meeting Agenda

A well-prepared agenda ensures time well-spent in the kick-off meeting by

1. giving a comprehensive overview of the budget project;
2. assuring that the right people attend;
3. ensuring that sufficient time exists between the issuance of the kick-off meeting agenda notice and the meeting date for members to come prepared to address the premeeting agenda action items;
4. assuring that everyone is prepared with their input;
5. identifying and orienting the budget team to the budget tools and how they are to be used (e.g., the accounting system, and any other set of tools your company uses for the budget cycle for establishing schedules and deadlines);
6. providing budget training dates and agenda for the budget training sessions; and
7. providing (or its location on the company network) the budget team with the budget process task list (see sample in Appendix A).

The above items appear to be a lot to do prior to a meeting. However, these items are not time intensive. They simply serve as a checklist for preparation for reducing meeting time.

The budget agenda has four parts:

1. Agenda items that provide guidelines for the budget cycle
2. Agenda items that require actions prior to the meeting
3. Agenda items that include action items for the next and subsequent budget meetings (discussed in the kick-off meeting)
4. New business

Action Item

THE MICROSOFT EXCEL WORKBOOK: If you are using the Microsoft Excel *Business Budget Builder* workbook with this book, ensure that you complete item 1 of STAGE I in the Getting Started tab. Completing this item first is critical for using the entire workbook. Item 2 Management Team corresponds with this chapter. Follow the directions at the top of the Management Team spreadsheet before completing the spreadsheet.

CHAPTER 3

Budget Schedule

Considering the budget as "extra work" minimizes its usefulness as a tool for success.

Beginning on the right track is the most important part of budgeting. If you plan to use the *Business Budget Builder* Microsoft Excel spreadsheet, select item 3 on the *Getting Started Menu*. Follow the directions in the budget Project Schedule spreadsheet for completing this spreadsheet.

Time is always an issue for any project that is as intense as budget development and execution. However, using project management principles diminishes the intensity of budgeting through organization. If organization for it falters at the outset, the budget cycle will prompt more complications and challenges during the process.

The Budget Project Schedule

Budgeting initially is a balancing act for the firm, like all other activities contributing to the company's success. It requires time, resources, and tasks definition. To make the budget cycle successful, treat it like any other operational project. If your company has never undertaken a budging cycle, the guidance of this book will minimize the learning curve. The practice of project management reduces the learning curve through a clearly laid out method that defines:

- Tasks—A listing of all the tasks necessary for completing and executing the budget. See Appendix A for a comprehensive list.
- Timeline—The timeline is a calendar populated with the budgeted tasks, milestones, critical paths, and deadlines all

reflected on the budget project calendar. However, allocating this period of time reduces intensity and allows a smooth integration of the budget process into other operational activities.

- Resources—Resources includes human, equipment, and materials toward completing and executing the budget.
- Milestones—Milestones are major accomplishments along the path of completing and implementing the budget. See Appendix A for a list of budget milestones to consider for the budget process.
- Deadlines—Established deadlines the budget team leader sets for staying on track for executing the budget. These deadlines correspond with identified milestones.

Remember that the above methodology simply adds structure to the planning process. Conference or meeting rooms are unnecessary, especially with IT technology and networks. Make use of such technology to reduce time in meetings and take advantage of applications that can speed up budget preparation.

The Budget Management Process

Chapter 1 highlighted the following three budget cycle segments:

1. Budget preplanning
2. Pro forma financial statements development
3. Budget execution

The budget process naturally flows from the strategic plan. However, if you do not engage in a strategic planning process, the budget becomes the company plan for a narrower period (1 year rather than the 3- to 5-year period the strategic plan would cover). The strategic plan has a greater scope, length of time planned, and breadth than the budgeting process. It is also much more intense and interactive, encompassing a much broader review of the external environment, company review, strategic development, and action plans for strategy implementation. If your company has not engaged in strategic planning, it would be a worthwhile endeavor for setting sights beyond 1 year. Dr. Gary May has written an excellent book for learning more about implementing a strategic plan in your business called *Strategic Planning: Fundamentals for Small Business* by Business Expert Press.

A Budget Management Checklist

Whoever assumes budget responsibility in your organization has overall responsibility for budget development and execution. This section provides a checklist for getting started on the budget.

1. Selecting and implementing project management applications
2. Setting up the project tasks, resources, and acquisition of the necessary material and equipment resources
3. Preparing and maintaining the agenda and subsequent meeting agendas required for the project
4. Chairing all project meetings
5. Tracking and reporting on progress
6. Assigning action items as needed and conducting follow-up prior to meetings
7. Updating the project schedule
8. Drawing the project to a close
9. Preparing and distributing monthly financial performance status reports with highlights and variances
10. Preparing for the next budget cycle
11. Reviewing project budget performance status meeting
12. Documenting and reporting budget performance
13. Assigning and tracking of action items
14. Analyzing the key challenges and lessons-learned sessions
15. Analyzing corrective actions related to budget performance
16. Re-forecasting coordination as required

CHAPTER 4

Objectives, Performance, and Measurements

Scattershot results from not having a clear target shot. Measuring scattershot is highly difficult for taking your best shot.

Objectives

After reading this chapter, you will be able to

1. identify and create specific objectives; and
2. identify a project plan for implementing objectives and their respective revenue, capital, or expenses.

Measuring Business Performance

Objectives are a logical starting point for the budget. All components of the business come under the scrutiny of the budget as the benchmark for financial performance. In his book on the Balanced Scorecard concerning a mechanism for performance and results, Paul Nevin suggests that communication is an essential element for success. He identifies at least six communication goals for development and implementation in keeping score of business endeavors:[1]

1. Awareness at all levels of the organization
2. Education of concepts
3. Engagement and commitment
4. Encouragement of participation
5. Enthusiasm generation
6. Effective and rapid dissemination of results

Objectives are the means of communicating performance results through your company. They also engage commitment, ownership, and participation of what the business wants to accomplish. Objectives also point to results.

The budget would be incomplete without a performance measurement segment, and objectives are the bases for performance measurement. Any activity in the company needs measuring to determine progress. Performance reviews occur at various time intervals and levels in the business. The primary performance review is financial statements reporting. These occur monthly, quarterly, and at year-end. The budget is an integral part of the financial statements. They measure financial performance against established objectives. The financial statements express some of the objectives you set during the budget cycle, such as sales revenue, the aging of accounts receivables and payables, gross margin, and net earnings. This means that all three financial statements come under review at the stated periods.

Baseline and Objectives

Objectives provide a greater degree of confidence in and control over the budget numbers than projecting from a baseline. The baseline is where your business is based on prior performance and before setting objectives. Historical financials as a baseline provide a basis for future performance but not a guarantee for it. Markets and the economy change. Managing from a baseline can keep a company in a comfort zone and status quo. Objectives force a company beyond the comfort zone.

Objectives also aid you to work through uncertainties and risks confronting your business. Since objectives are proactive actions, they engage and review uncertainties and risks prior to the formulation of an objective. This book encourages an organizational and processes review along with markets assessment for determining where and how to strengthen the business to meet the market demands. While economic and marketplace uncertainties cannot be eliminated, such an approach enables the business to better prepare to meet them.

The budget sets quantifiable targets related to the strategic plan for its first year, such as specific revenues, gross margin, and net profit. These targets consider not only sales projections but also your current business status—whether your business caters to a microniche market (one location within one or two locales), a regional niche market (multilocations within a metropolitan area), or a state or nationwide market with sights set on more locations, markets, or channels.

Five Levels of Performance Evaluation

Objectives drive your business. All the market research, industry analysis, and historical trends examination are limited in terms of providing you with a well-defined marketing and sales budget. While these factors serve as bases for objectives, the objectives themselves provide the proactive targets for measuring where you want to be at the conclusion of your budgeted period.

Objectives also provide your company with performance incentives. Performance measurements for sales drive objectives for all supporting components of the company from the organizational to the individual level and include the following.

Total Business Performance

How well does the business perform compared to mission, strategy, and objectives? Within this context is where interpretive knowledge of the financial statements and other nonfinancial data come into focus. Financial ratios measure financial performance. However, there must be a comparative basis for such measurements. One basis is external and another is internal. The external consists of similar companies in the same industry. The internal consists of historical performance. Together they provide powerful tools for measuring how well your business performs against stated objectives. Chapter 15 guides you through two dimensions of statements review and highlights other metrics for financial performance.

Managing the business and its performance takes more than just the financial statements. The key to total business and financial performance evaluation is knowledge. Financial management is just one component of knowledge management (KM), but it is a critical one. KM has rapidly grown over a decade as a discipline for tapping into the entire set of business intelligence assets within the enterprise for making data relevant.[2]

Companies like Ernst & Young and Oracle provide solutions tools for integrating KM in larger companies for financial and nonfinancial performance measurement.[3] Such solution tools give CEOs and CFOs immediate access to desired data on business performance for quick and more informed decision-making that would otherwise be labor intensive, cumbersome, and perhaps even too late for responding to the market.[4]

Small and medium businesses have just as much a need for enterprise-wide knowledge as larger ones, especially for those on the cusp of breaking through to the next level of growth. For small-to-medium businesses, a full-scale KM implementation may not be feasible or for that matter useful. However, having a goal of database integration or linking of applications can improve productivity and decision-making, especially for an acquisition of an existing business in which disparate data warehouse systems exist. KM integration remains a realistic goal on a smaller scale for more efficient data storage and retrieval. In addition, streamlining KM could be preventive medicine for addressing the 10 business challenges solved through budgeting discussed in Chapter 1.

Total business performance rests on both financial and nonfinancial metrics within the KM environment.[5] KM provides a business with the capacity to manage the entire business as well as its component parts, particularly the supply chain, markets, channels, and distribution.[6] The key to KM or intellectual capital begins with the company's mission.[7] One critical measurement of the mission statement is the financial statements as well as ancillary financial and nonfinancial reports related to them.

Given that the financial statements are static snapshots, total business performance needs wider measurements than the financial statements. These measurements consist of nonfinancial metrics. The sections in this chapter, "Components of Objectives" and "Best Practice Measurements," discuss such metrics in more depth.

Having a knowledge data warehouse in place for budget participants and their staff to access lends to greater budget and business success. In a large number of small-and-medium-sized companies, many disconnected components make up the data warehouse, lending to inefficiency in data storage and retrieval. For this reason, a business also needs to consider budget for its KM and access to it for budget team members as well as all staff.

Matt Stevens, a 30-year construction management veteran and consultant to the industry, writes:

> Senior Managers must have a laser-like focus on financial matters. It affects every aspect of a business. Not knowing enough can lead to a slow but steady downward spiral. All activities expand or curtail due to money. Adopting technology, hiring, office expansion and bidder list qualification just to name a few. Well-managed firms keep clients, attract talent, and build value for its owners.[8]

He cites senior managers relative to financial matters. It is also important to recognize that knowledge of financial data must be commensurate with organizational and processes management at any level. That is, staff at all levels must have adequate knowledge appropriate for performing their work. Both leadership and adequate performance evaluation depend on it.

"Laser-like focus" at all levels drives total business performance. Superior business performance means that managers must have a dual focus: their respective organization and the overall business. They must also communicate this focus to their respective staff so that all individuals at all levels recognize their contribution on the entire business.

Budget participation, oversight, and performance outcomes mean that participants need not only access to data but also the knowledge to interpret it. Adequate performance evaluation derives from such oversight of KM. Inadequate KM can lead to systemic issues that can distort staff performance evaluation and influence morale. In other words, inadequate or disconnected data warehousing and retrieval can result in greater errors that are systemic and not necessarily staff related. Greater error rate, as Stevens reminds us, "can lead to a slow but steady spiral."

For these reasons, the budget must consider KM high on the priority list. KM done right is really a strategic initiative that could span several years. Dividing an implementation into fiscal periods makes its integration into the business achievable and a realistic goal. Setting up performance expectations for each implementation milestone for systems and staff can provide your company with how well you do with what you have at the conclusion of each fiscal period. Setting such expectations can also inform management if it needs additional KM systems and tools for driving efficiency and growth.

Executive Performance

Budget managers play a critical role in the performance of the total business. Their compensation can relate to such performance. Developing governance criteria not only on the executive level but also on the organizational level is essential not only for managing to stated goals but also for organization and process improvements. Managerial budget responsibility involves company constituents both inside and outside the company. Budget managers have a hand in managing certain constituents. The sales organization manages customers, internal staff, and certain vendors. The manufacturing organization manages internal staff and suppliers, while having a hand in customer management through support. Budget managers share management responsibility for company constituents, demonstrating how organizations within the company depend on one another. How well each does this task influences overall business performance and contributes to financial performance. Such interdependency suggests that a peer performance review provides a more realistic judgment on performance in addition to direct report review. Both provide a multidimensional review based on collaborative efforts and total contribution to the company as seen through several sets of eyes. How well each manager manages his or her organization influences the work of other managers and the company as a whole.

Since budget management is a collaborative effort among peers, budget team members contribute to establishing management criteria that measure their own performance. These criteria become a shared set of knowledge for setting performance expectations throughout the company. The criteria assume access to the knowledge base containing that criteria and a means of adequate reporting on both financial and nonfinancial performance, such as financial reports and established nonfinancial metrics.

Key Management Area (KMA) Management Performance

The calling out of KMAs for performance review illustrates that they are fundamental and essential links in a well-managed organization. Management of defined KMAs can identify weak links in the organization where resources may need addressing for meeting efficiency or performance objectives. For example, do inventory cycle counts show an unacceptable level of variances? This could lead to a year-end physical inventory issue during an audit and produce a materiality problem unless addressed earlier under the KMA of vendor management. The same holds true for other KMAs, such as customer management, channel management, and material requirements management.

While individual and organizational component performance reviews go together, they are separate and distinct. KMA review focuses on business performance and improvements, while individual review focuses on staff performance (including managerial). They can become confused so that employees sometimes receive an evaluation based on systemic issues. Identifying them as distinct allows your business to identify core issues for appropriate solutions for fine-tuning resources and making them more effective. KMA performance reviews can be very informal and a continuing evaluation throughout the budget year.

Those involved in the KMA, such as inventory management, would normally be the ones engaged in evaluating its current performance and determining where performance improvements could be made. For example, implementing an integrated material requirements planning (MRP) and inventory management could not only improve production performance but also reduce shipment time and improve product quality, while reducing frustration. Those involved in the current systems are important for identifying specification requirements. The budget manager works with them for project budget costs and an implementation schedule. This project then becomes part of the budget objectives and plan.

Constituent Performance

A company wants to ensure that all constituents integrate into the business strategy and stated objectives. Having a year-end performance review for constituents ensures this.

For example, vendor performance is critical to customer product delivery and satisfaction. All vendors must align with company strategy and objectives for total supply chain management and customer retention. Have they met the criteria stated in agreements? Has the company managed these agreements well? Such an examination also applies to other constituents such as financial institutions and employees. Do banks meet the requirements you have for cash management, funding, and related services? Do you have criteria for banking services for supporting your company's financial management requirements? Future selections depend on performance evaluation. They are the vendor and you are their customer. Having criteria initially for banking selection allows you to not only make a selection that supports your business but also aid in evaluating how well they perform in this endeavor. Constituent performance review has several purposes. Some purposes for material vendors include

1. to determine if the constituent has a drag on performance;
2. to determine the best mix of vendor selection for sole-source or multi-sourcing;
3. to meet material requirements criteria and integration of vendor performance into total product quality and delivery;
4. to provide a competitive environment among vendors for technological advances, pricing, delivery, customer benefit, and product performance; and
5. to determine the best team players and partners for your business. (You could also outsource warranty and technical support services and may want to ensure they are best fit for customer support.)

Individual Performance

Staff performance is vital for their integration and participation in their respective organization and the company as a whole. Their involvement in establishing objectives gives them ownership and incentive for accomplishment. When this occurs during the budget cycle, they will not encounter surprises at period appraisals in terms of their contribution to company objectives. In addition, they will be able to enjoy viewing the larger picture of company strategy. They also realize growth and compensation as the company grows.

Review Chapter 12 for best practices related to individual performance for roles and responsibilities. It identifies key areas critical to establishing sound criteria for performance: job descriptions, objectives, and performance measurements. Performance evaluation is a budget issue for two reasons. First, compensation is a budgetary matter. Second, if criteria are not in place, budget planning is the time for allocating funds for their implementation. For these reasons, the consideration of individual performance evaluation has direct economic impact for the business and needs addressing up front. This happens through the staffing plan.

Components of Objectives

Objectives have five components. Three of these components are measurement components, while the other two are feasibility components. Feasibility indicates whether they are sufficiently reasonable and practical for acting as a measurement for performance. These components consist of the following:

1. Specificity—Identifies what you want to accomplish. For example, open a new sales office in New York City for a base of operations to service and support growing customer base.
2. Measurability—Measurements quantify the objective with a specific value. How do you know when you completed the objective? What measuring stick or measurement criteria will you use? You may wish to establish more than one criterion for objective fulfillment. Some sample criteria for the illustration in point 1 above could be

   a. to lease a 20,000 square foot space to accommodate fulfillment and warranty;
   b. to hire administrative and technical staff; and
   c. to begin warranty service for customers on 01/01/20xx.

Objectives can be set at various levels with their corresponding measurements: strategic and operating. A strategic objective is similar to the example used above for expansion to a new location. A major operating objective for a retail store may be to reduce inventory shrinkage, that is, the amount and value of loss due to theft, oversight in receiving, or spoilage.

The store could set two metrics for this objective: (1) identify the percentage level for it, for example, from its current level of 1.99% of sales to 1.43% of sales and (2) determine the timeline, such as the close of the fiscal year. The percentage would translate into dollar savings the store would realize over the budgeted period. From this objective, the company would establish a plan of action and identify the resources necessary for accomplishing it, such as adjusting order points and performing onsite quality review of suppliers.

3. Achievability—Although part of objective setting, achievability as such is not a measurement. Rather it is a judgment about whether the objective should be undertaken. This criterion is more subjective rather than objective. Part of your evaluation for achievability would be your resources and their costs. These resources include staffing, equipment, subcontracting, and facilities. Another important element for achievability is timing. Will engaging this objective interfere with business operations or enhance it? What impact will it have on net income? Will it meet the company's mission? Achievability surfaces prior to setting measurements.

4. Realistic—Realism is another judgment call that sets a tolerance level for selecting an objective. Tolerances are a set of parameters, a bandwidth, or a range within which the event judged must fall for considering it acceptable. For example, the project cannot use more than available resources or it cannot exceed certain costs. In addition, it must generate a certain amount of revenue within the first year of operations. This calls for an examination of the market in that location.

5. Time related—This component simply refers to a completion date. The time-related component could also include stated milestones along the time-line identified by particular dates with events set to accomplish those milestones.

As you walk through the components, achievability and realism take precedent. Before completing the other three parts of objective setting (specificity, measurability, and time related), a judgment concerning its feasibility comes first. At this point, going through a checklist aids in this judgment call. Consider the following criteria questions and add some of your own:

1. Does it align with our core business thrust?
2. Do we want to undertake it during this budget cycle or at least begin it?
3. Does it match up with our strategies?
4. Do we have the resources to undertake it?

5. Will it provide a targeted return on investment?

6. Does it align with our organizational structure?

7. Will it help penetrate the market and accomplish our mission?

8. Will it increase our revenue stream and net profit?

9. Will the company recover capital outlays within a set timeframe?

10. Can we manage the objective from our primary location?

Best Practices Measurements

Developing scorecards as measurements for review give you vital information for continuous evaluation and improvements. The Balanced Scorecard method that Robert Kaplan and David Norton developed gave a way of evaluating and improving business performance. They challenged the "best-in-class" concept by bringing in performance measures for company vision and mission statement. Years later Paul Nevin tied vision to measurement and writes, "The scorecard is an essential device that translates vision into reality through the articulation of vision (and strategy)."[9] He outlines a series of questions that get a company from jargon and buzzwords to "using measurements to capture the correct balance of skills, processes, and customer requirements that lead to our desired financial future as reflected in the vision."[10] From the vision, the scorecard flows to measurements through strategies and objectives.[11] He stresses that not all objectives and their measurements are financial, but they "are not complete without financial measures of performance."[12] Using industry financial ratios as benchmarks of success as described in Chapter 15 actually gives you competitive objectives by using them as targets rather than simply as industry comparisons.

However, moving from the strictly financial arena to other nonfinancial segments of the organization requires other types of measurements. Nevin gives an example of focusing on "the customer's voice" from the various media available to you to gather critical information from them concerning your performance on their behalf.[13] Once you gather this information, your company can glean from it sufficient data for formulating ways of measuring customer retention. Nevin suggests several metrics for doing this, among which are complaints, loyalty, satisfaction, and duration of relationship.[14] Develop your own measurements based on your company's experience and from researching industry data.

Mark Graham Brown discusses how to prepare measurements in different organizations of the company as well as for service industry companies for driving performance. In one specific example, he cites Browning-Ferris Industries (BFI). To prevent losing customers, it had to develop measurements that catered to their retention: timeliness, quiet trucks, undamaged cans, and all garbage collected. Of course, costs were involved in developing and implementing such measurements. However, so was revenue (i.e., the loss of it).[15] Therefore, a company cannot dismiss nonfinancial metrics for measuring performance. The performance measured influences the financial statements. Brown recommends limiting performance measurements to six categories:[16]

1. Financial (Financial Management)
2. Product and service quality (Vendor Management, Inventory Management)
3. Suppliers (Vendor Management)
4. Customer satisfaction (Customer Management)
5. Process and operational (All areas)
6. Employee satisfaction (All areas)

These are useful categories, because they encompass all areas of the company. The discussion that follows ties these categories to the practices brought out in Chapters 5 and 6 and selected appendices. In parenthesis beside each categories 1–6 above are corresponding KMAs this book identifies and discusses in Chapter 7. Although Brown talks about measures and performance separate from objectives, objectives themselves encompass measurement of performance as a criterion. Review the topic in this chapter, under the section "Components of Objectives," for a more in-depth discussion of measurement as a component of an objective. As measurements surface from objectives, the particular metric arises as a specific quantifier for an objective.

One essential measurement Brown omits in his list is Treasury. While Treasury falls under the purview of Finance, it is sufficiently important to call out and treat separately much like capital budgeting, which is a separate entity in the budget. Capital budgeting encompasses the entire company and thereby requires a coordinated effort. Treasury likewise has a similar position. It encompasses most of the balance sheet and the organizations in the company the balance sheet touches. Treasury engages three important constituents that need separate treatment: banking, other lenders, and investors. They need management just as much as the funding from them. Managing the relationship with them gains their support as an advisory arm for your company. Furthermore, they could also supply you with valuable tools for improving cash management. Consider preparing a checklist of the services and features your company requires from a financial institution or bank when the time arrives for selecting another bank. Make your selection based on such criteria.

In addition, Treasury also pinpoints a vital standard or metric for the business that needs special attention for it to be flexible in its money management and financial leverage—the company's credit rating. Without a sound credit rating, a company's flexibility for expansion projects would be highly limited and restricted. Maintaining a sound credit rating provides your company the mechanism not only for negotiating better lending terms but also for attracting equity investors. Both view your ability in financial management as an indispensable criterion for providing you funding. Thinking through objectives for cash management and laying out corresponding measures and action plans for it lends to a sounder foundation for the other listed categories. Furthermore, resources cost for such action plans needs identification in the budget.

The category of Finance is appropriately number one on Brown's list. Sound financial management reaches into every organization in the company through accounting, planning, budgeting, and internal controls. Chapters 13–15 specifically address financial management and performance in detail under the topics of developing the pro forma financial statements, budget execution, and financial performance reviews. Figure 15.3 in Chapter 15 consists of the most common financial ratios for use with financial statements analysis. Financial ratios measure and benchmark business performance. Financial ratios also act as metrics for measuring financial strengths and weaknesses.

Review Appendix C for identifying vendor management practices for product or service quality and suppliers or vendor objectives and their measurements. This appendix provides useful information for evaluating vendor performance. This information also aids in determining whether that performance adequately supports you and your customers. Appendix B complements Appendix C with best practices for customer relations, retention, and improved communications. Addressing the questions posed under "Records Management" in Appendix B will guide you toward measuring customer management. Give attention to the recommended best practices often omitted while interacting with customers. Ensuring they are in place builds stronger relationships with customers. Customer benchmarking is another area in which you can set an objective or initiative for determining how well you serve the customer:

1. Customer service
2. Customer satisfaction
3. Competitive benchmarks
4. Financial performance related to customer management

Consider the four major areas of benchmarking mentioned in Appendix B for initiatives to be budgeted.

This book stresses the need for organization and processes review as part of the budget process. This is what Brown identifies as the process and operational category. Chapters 5 and 6 discuss how to go about a review of the company's overall organization and corresponding processes. The goal is to strengthen them with direction, safeguards, and focus on the customer, communications, and resources management. As you read these chapters, work through the questionnaires, and complete the action items, identify and list no more than three to four objectives for addressing issues and improvements for supporting customer retention.

Action Items

1. Have each budget manager review Chapters 5–7 concerning organization, processes, and KMAs. Do any organizational or process issues arise to the surface needing improvement? Are there any risks issues that need addressing through objectives? Identify what type

of performance you want to measure within your organization and their corresponding processes and KMAs.

2. Quantify the performance you would like to realize. For example, you want to identify the current levels of product returns or warranty repairs. What would be an acceptable level for the beginning of the budget period and for the end of the budget period? You may want to consult some organizations that perform benchmarking to determine if they have benchmarks for the performance areas you want to consider. Visit The Benchmarking Network for research conducted that you may wish to use to measure specific areas of your business, for example, customer satisfaction.

CHAPTER 5

Organizational Review

The secret of all victory lies in the organization of the non-obvious.
—Marcus Aurelius, Roman Emperor, 121–180 AD

Objectives

After completing this chapter, you will be able to accomplish the following toward the budget process:

1. Conduct an organizational structure integrity review for ensuring that the fundamentals of the business underlying the budget come under review for determining the budget costs associated with them for their improvement and performance.
2. Identify resources and risks management issues and the necessary applications for internal controls and safeguards for considering their costs.

Conducting an Organizational Review

The first item on the agenda is business organization. In planning the business, the fundamentals can easily escape notice or taken for granted to the detriment of the firm. If business gets the fundamentals right, then all that flows from them make it easier to build upon them in an efficient manner from budgeting to market execution.

Beginning with the basics lays a strong plan foundation. Businesses, like any other type of group, organize around a specific mission, goals, and tasks. Coming to grips with three fundamental building blocks of the business—organization, processes, and money—can help structure the company around them.

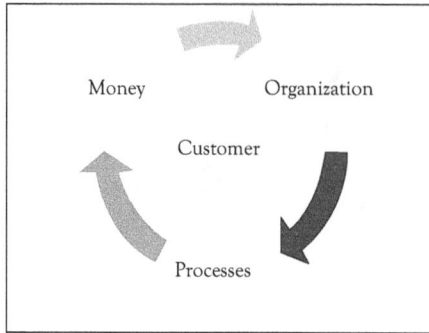

Figure 5.1. Fundamental organizational components.

The illustration in Figure 5.1 shows these three business building blocks. They include structure as defined by an organization chart. They consist of processes that define movement and activities through which the structure delivers products and services to the customer. An organization is in business for the customer. These processes make up the control (managerial) environment for the budget and its execution.

Rose Hightower describes the control environment as the "indicator of the level of control consciousness of the company."[1] She afterward expands on this, "It is the basis for all the other components providing direction, discipline, and structure."[2] The organizational chart symbolizes the business structure. Its processes give direction for business transactions and internal controls for addressing the risks that businesses encounter.

Money for funding the structure and processes make up the third building block. This funding comes from sales revenue, debt, or investment. Subsequent chapters address each of these funding sources. The marketing and sales plan discussed in Chapter 8 is, of course, the major source of funding growth. Debt financing requirements come into play for strategic initiatives, line of credit for financing seasonal businesses, or other operating objectives to sustain cash flow when the bulk of expected revenues occur farther out, such as in viticulture, ranching, or certain retail stores. Investment financing includes additional paid-in-capital, private equity placement, or initial public offering to address greater expansion than is currently possible with existing available capital. An initial organizational review for setting objectives addresses these three building blocks. Underestimating the basics of business can lead business managers down a roadway littered with potholes.

A business with dislocated or disjointed practices, processes, and organizational structures are costly and prone to fraud, theft, and other losses. They interrupt communications, promote in-fighting and empire building, and cause tension to rise. Focusing on business fundamentals helps prevent these disruptions. Furthermore, getting the various functions of the business to champion the customer gives them a rallying point. Consequently, it is important to review the three building blocks for determining gaps and weaknesses for better service to the customer. This chapter and the next give guidance for that review.

A well-defined organization has three major managerial components: (1) structure, (2) resources management and safeguards, and (3) leadership. A well-established organizational structure helps to view the full scope of managing productive resources toward developing and delivering products and services to customers.

Structure: Challenges and Evolution over Time

In the early stages of the budget process, the company should evaluate the adequacy of its structural makeup. The intent of this book is to point out the importance of a review of structural components for attending to cracks in the integrity of the business. This review is also important for identifying actions and costs to close those cracks. This integrity review includes

1. management and management activities;
2. risks exposure;
3. financial information systems and reporting; and
4. performance measurements.

Organizational Structure Integrity Review

Below are some tips for conducting a review during the budget preplanning stage for each of the above-listed fundamentals of the business.

Management and Management Activities

Review the "tone at the top" of the organization chart. In its *Audit Committee Brief*, Deloitte LLP noted, "Management's tone at the top is an essential element of effective internal control and corporate governance."[3]

This tone is as important in budgeting as it is in comprehensive governance. They are two sides of the same coin. Although tone emphasizes integrity and ethics, it also points to commitment and priority. Leadership champions processes and commitment to them because it realizes that they safeguard assets and integrity. If organization and processes receive secondary importance, managers at every level will sense it and give similar priority to them. Laxity in essential safeguards could be indicative of laxity in ethics. Rose Hightower links evaluation of "tone at the top" to "interruption to operations and money."[4] A breakdown or lack of internal controls lends to greater risks over assets and become costly. Consequently, they need addressing as budgetary components.

Risks Assessment and Exposure

Evaluation of risks to the business carries its own rewards. Risk areas in the business include more than financial risks, although they have financial repercussions. A company needs to give priority to preventive measures against fraud, theft, embezzlement, and other losses across the entire organization during the budget preplanning stage. Such losses are unplanned and could cause costly surprises, if not addressed up front. Are sufficient control mechanisms in place for insuring risks reduction? Among those that need consideration are written policies and procedures, financial performance reviews, segregation of duties, and security over assets.

The budget acts as a significant risk assessment tool when it includes review of organizational structural components as segregation of duties, policies, and procedures. After assessing risks and establishing risks management, you can draft up a plan of action for each and identify costs associated with that plan for your budget.

Financial Information Systems and Reporting

The backbone of financial management is the accounting system and its reporting capability. It provides tracking, feedback, and financial measurement. It is not only a tool but also a control mechanism when set up and used properly. At a minimum, the accounting system should be able to do the following:

1. Report on the three accounting periods: historical, current activities, and pro forma development (budgets)
2. Financial statements analysis capability
3. Sound general ledger and journals management
4. Provide for closing prior periods that prevent prior period postings and misstating period financial statements
5. Control access to sensitive financial data on various levels that allow for segregation of duties
6. Accommodate business requirements, such as inventory management, multiuser access, and loan and fixed asset tracking
7. Manage constituents
8. User friendliness for a rapid learning curve in training
9. Work flow guidance that corresponds with accounting and financial management practices
10. Capable of integrating ancillary applications necessary for full financial management

Performance Measurements

The budget cycle is the venue for reviewing, designing, and developing performance measurements for the budgeted year. Performance measurements include financial performance, governance performance, constituent performance, and individual performance. Objectives should be for both nonfinancial and financial performance so that scores can be associated with them for measuring success.[6] Before the budget team even begins discussing numbers, it must prepare company objectives. Objectives determine the financial numbers and often include financial performance.

Budgeting Risks Management and Safeguards

Current and future business activity depends on the management of resources in a manner that leads toward optimizing greater revenue generation and profits. The budget should account for segregation of duties when considering revenue performance, controls, and safeguards. Resource management, risks reduction, and marketing opportunities work hand in hand.

The segregation of duties as a resource and risks management mechanism is a matter of business priority for proper safeguards over the business. Smaller companies and firms may not have sufficient staff for allocating work. In this case, the company must decide on the extent of segregation of duties for risks exposure reduction. In doing so, it will need to recognize the impact on the company that its priorities place on risks to revenue. Risks exposure could result in weaknesses in safeguarding assets and costs to revenue and make the company prone to fraud or theft.

The Committee of Sponsoring Organizations of the Treadway Commission (COSO) raises a sense of urgency for giving attention to proper safeguards. It identifies the framework for safeguards as key risk indicators (KRIs) and defines them as "metrics used by organizations to provide an early signal of increasing risk exposures in various areas of the enterprise."[7] A company needs to decide on the level of priority it gives to the segregation of duties for insuring proper risk management. The lower the priority the higher the company has risk exposure. Without this priority, the company could throw up roadblocks to market opportunity and corresponding revenue.[8]

Segregation of duties prevents losses due to fraud or theft. Poor segregation of duties could mean a reallocation of financial resources from marketing and revenue-producing activities to cover fraud or theft losses. The budget process is the place where budget managers review trade-offs and negotiate against the risks of whether the costs of additional resources will generate greater revenue or expose the company to weaknesses in safeguards.

Outsourcing is an alternative to assuming more internal staff. The CFO or finance manager should have this issue at the top of the budgeting agenda for discussion during the preplanning budget phase. This priority allows each budget manager to think through staffing and equipment requirements to meet marketing and sales efforts and to maintain sound risk management.

Leadership: Directing Resources and Accomplishment

Leadership plays an integral part in organizational management. Leadership directs resources toward accomplishing objectives, establishing management controls, setting the mission and goals, and creating an environment for innovation. Budget leadership has two parts to it: responsibility and accountability. Responsibility leads certain business components, tasks, and capital resources that include staffing, equipment, and materials for production. Responsibility includes scope of management and decision-making authority for the acquisition and application of resources toward business objectives and sales and marketing efforts.

Accountability identifies the accounting for performance of resources toward business mission and objectives. The budget is the financial benchmark for this performance. Without a budget, the business will have little to guide it for measuring performance in the application of funds. The budget identifies business targets and the costs for carrying them out. A budget manager ensures that the segment of business over which the leader has oversight performs within specified measurements as defined by objectives and limited by the funds required to gain and retain customers.

Action Items

The Organizational Integrity Review

The budget is the time to conduct an examination of the four elements of the organizational structure integrity review:

1. Management and management activities
2. Risks assessment and exposure
3. Financial information systems and reporting
4. Performance measurements

This part of the budget is critical because each of the four elements lead to a reality check for the preparedness of the company to engage the market as well as identify revenue- or cost-related issues. Without this examination, the real budget cost encounters uncertainty. Furthermore, such a reality check prevents "quick fixes" and fire fighting until such a time when the company can afford to address needed organizational challenges and issues. They could also affect the development of realistic pro forma financial statements.

Management and Management Activities

The first elements of "management and management activities" drive the other three. This makes the examination of governance a top priority for two reasons. Referring back to the Deloitte LLP *Audit Committee Brief* is helpful at this point. Management not only sets the tone for internal control and corporate governance but also is the underlying principle for "employee and investor confidence" and for maintaining "corporate integrity."[9] Employee and investor confidence along with corporate integrity may not appear related to the budgetary numbers. However, they are, and they have a significant impact on the entire budget process and the financial well-being of the company. Next to the customer, employees and investors are important constituents, and their confidence in the management of the company has a cost. This management encompasses sound internal controls without which gaps in financial management could permit losses from fraud, theft, and cost management.

Action Item. Review your organization chart and determine which KMAs you currently outsource. Notate them on the organizational chart as outsourced. Make a list (if you do not already have one) of all outsource contracts and the contract cost of each one (see example in Table 5.1). This list will not include vendors who provide product materials but only those for repairs, maintenance, facilities upkeep, and related outsourced contracts. Note expiration dates, pricing, and other contractual arrangement affecting your budget. Your accounting system may already accommodate vendor outsource contract tracking so that preparing a report may provide you with the information needed for identifying all outsourcing contract pricing. If not, this may be an additional system feature or application you may wish to budget for tracking contracts and their costs.

Costs of replacement parts not covered under maintenance agreements may not be included in the contract price. This is where evaluation of your current capital equipment as part of your capital plan becomes useful. Would it be cost effective to budget newly leased equipment (under a capital or operating lease) given the life of existing equipment, or perform an outright purchase of new or used equipment?

The question of financing arises for this decision and would need to be factored into cost of capital. Working with the CFO or Controller

Table 5.1. Outsourcing Contract Costs

Contract number	Vendor	Purpose	Expiration	Total price

integrates financing into a total company capital plan and its corresponding costs of capital and depreciation expenses.

If there are organizational components currently not on the organizational chart, enter them. Designate those that are outsourced. Do you want to continue to outsource them or manage them internally? Draw up a transition plan and corresponding expense allocation if you plan to make them internal. For outsourced organizational components, review them according to the Outsourcing Vendor Criteria in Table C.1 of Appendix C.

CHAPTER 6

Processes Review

A good roadmap will get you to your destination.

Objectives

After completing this chapter, you will be able to accomplish the following toward the budget process:

1. Conduct a business processes review for better identifying staffing, capital, and materials resources for their management and funding.
2. Identify if the internal controls adequately manage processes for product and services delivery
3. Review necessary steps and funding needed for insuring adequate controls.

Processes as the Basis for Productivity and Funding

If a company concentrates simply on organization, it could omit critical funding for resources that drive processes. Organizational management and processes development inextricably tie together. Organization assumes processes for driving efficiency, cost reduction, and safeguards for the business. More often than not, many small-to-medium businesses do not always clarify processes through established written policies and procedures. As a result, they miss many cost reduction and productivity measures through improvement potential (or Kaizen).

Processes evaluation is a preventive measure for safeguarding assets and company confidential and proprietary information. Costs for clarification of processes and corresponding internal controls go a long way to prevent greater losses such as increased insurance premiums and the time, money, and energy toward the purchase of replacements. Without such clarification, budgets for resource requirements are difficult to ascertain. Processes are closer to the applied resources than the organization chart.

Processes guide productive resources. The organization simply identifies where the human, capital, and material resources belong. Stepping through business processes helps the company to identify resource requirements and their corresponding costs more thoroughly for both product development and production. If the company has not clarified processes and their management resource requirements, their funding could be hit and miss. Surprises could arise during the course of the fiscal year if a business component within the company discovers that it omitted specific resources for a process.

The Process Questionnaire in Table 6.1 serves as a guide for budget managers during the budget kick-off meeting. This questionnaire calls for

Table 6.1. Processes Questionnaire

Process questionnaire
1. Is there a champion in the company for processes definition and development?
2. Are all the processes in the company well defined with policies and procedures?
3. Which processes in the company need better clarification?
4. Does a given process fit in the overall organizational schematic and integrate well with it?
5. Are processes in the company well staffed?
6. Is there overlap or duplication in processes?
7. Which processes are outsourced?
8. Has the company created specific criteria for the outsourced process?
9. Is there a negotiated agreement in place for the outsourced process?
10. Is there an internal staff person who oversees the outsourced process agreement?
11. Does the outsourced entity have proper credentials, licensing, liability insurance, and bonding required for managing the process?
12. Does the outsourced entity understand where it fits in the company's overall organization chart?
13. Does the outsourced entity for the process have a clearly defined management structure for elevating issues and problems for the outsourced process?
14. Does equipment support organizational processes?
15. Does the company need to reorganize for increased productivity?
16. Where are processes that have risk exposure (i.e., where fraud and other losses could occur)?

budget managers to review their processes requirements for budget preparation and execution. Funding requirements do not materialize until the completion of this review. It asks managers to consider the driving forces supporting their organizational effectiveness toward the company's overall mission.

Reviewing Processes

Processes work within the organization and identify movement of activity, control points for work, and the necessary steps for defining, developing, and delivering products and services. The financial statements account for and report on financial transactions for all process events. For example, both the balance sheet and income statement report on inventory, materials movements through work in process, and direct and indirect labor. However, if financial management stopped at historical financial statements reporting, lack of measurements for successfully attaining the business mission could cause the company to roam into undefined waters.

The budget measures processes efficiency and productivity. In setting specific pro forma financial statements ratio targets, they serve to measure the efficiency and productivity of processes. These ratios act as key performance indicators (KPIs). They measure the success of the organization in maximizing targeted revenues, gross profit, and net margin through business processes. However, there are two sets of KPIs you would want to consider, both of which are indicators of sound processes: financial ratios and nonfinancial metrics. Table 6.2 provides examples of financial ratios and metrics that give indicators of process performance and efficiency challenges.[1] The Benchmark Ratio/Metric column is the established measurement for the activity. For more on financial ratios and their application, read Chapter 15.

Reviewing business processes for adequacy of internal controls incurs costs, time, and material. However, internal controls are the mechanism for risk management. As part of the budget process, risk management aids in reducing theft, embezzlement, fraud, and other losses. Risk management focuses on weak control points and areas in processes where such risks are most prevalent.

Table 6.2. Ratios and Metrics for Identifying Process Issues for Improvement

Sample KPIs
(For the benchmark, enter competitive industry benchmarks or those used internally)

Financial ratio	Benchmark ratio/metric	Best practice process measured
Accounts Receivable Turnover: [Annual credit sales/Average A/R]		Collections: These ratios could be indicators of inefficiency of collections due to systemic or insufficient resources. They could also refer to lack of credit checks performed.
Average Collection Period: [365/A/R turnover]		
Sales to Fixed Assets: [Sales/Fixed Assets]		Equipment Use: This ratio could indicate equipment upkeep, equipment age, demand to capacity, or materials lead-time. Review these areas for process challenges.
Direct Materials to Sales: [Direct materials/Sales]		Vendor Management: Do you have a multisourcing policy? Review vendor contracts for compliance; review impacts on pricing and delivery costs. Review overall vendor management.
Direct Labor to Sales: [Direct labor/sales]		Workforce Management: Are there clearly defined job descriptions that reduce activity overlap? Review overtime rate and capacity. Do they reflect a proper ratio of labor to work in process based on your benchmark?
Inventory Turnover: [COGS/Average Inventory]		Sales/Fulfillment/Inventory Status: Review sales to plan and sales per sales person. Review stock status, lead times, returns, warranty fulfillment; obsolescence (E&O)

Metric	Benchmark ratio/metric	Best practice process measured
Returns on Orders		Quality Assurance: Review defects and shipment process (drop shipment versus direct); review RMA process both in timeliness/speed and completeness.
Warranty Fulfillment/Satisfaction		
Inventory Cycle Count Error Rate		WIP Process and Documentation: Review bill of material and work order process through WIP; review rework and scrap process; review count procedures and financial accounting system accuracy.

Performing a review from a project perspective is a best practice that can better identify the costs associated with internal controls implementation for any area of the business. Identifying and applying metrics and using an operational dashboard with project management enable you to track process deficiencies and set up a project for corrective action.[2] Business processes projects can be multifiscal year endeavors. For this reason, if the company has resources available, the selection of a project manager for risk management would be an efficient means for internal controls implementation. Smaller companies may not have such resources. In this case, such an endeavor would fall within the scope of the CFO for drawing up a plan identifying, designing, and implementing best practice internal controls. BWise, Inc. recommends a four-step process for implementing internal controls risks management:[3]

1. Preparation—Milestones, targeted goals, methodology, content, involvement, and top management commitment.
2. Implementation—Scope and project plan and start time.
3. Roll out—Security, technical support, linkage to existing systems, IT infrastructure issues, and training.
4. Live—Monitoring and change management board.

Laying these out in a project plan would make it easier to identify a budget for the targeted budgeting period.

Table 6.3 shows 12 business practices that strengthen the organization for contributing to value and improved product and service delivery. These practices ensure that continuous improvement takes place in the organization when business managers constantly apply them. The budget identifies the measurements for process improvements for driving increased revenues or cost reductions.

Although business policies and procedures for processes require costs to implement, they provide the parameters for efficiency and help reduce business risks such as fraud or theft that drive up insurance expenses and replacement costs. Rose Hightower states that financial risks occur when gaps exist in internal control procedures. Such gaps lend to an opportunity for "fraud or misuse" of resources.[4] Giving secondary priority to preventive measures that lend to losses also influence the ability to obtain debt or equity funding.

Table 6.3. *Organizational Business Practices*

Organizational business practices
1. Communicate expectations: do your vendors, customers, employees, and bankers know how you conduct business so they can support you? What needs improving? How?
2. Establish business routines: do they lend to quality production of products and services? For example, they have second reviews, inspection of products, documentation, and transactions. This holds true whether the business is manufacturing, retail, or a professional service.
3. Prepare systems that lend to efficient product and service delivery and the shortest route (critical path) through processes.
4. Safeguard and maintain business assets through defined policies.
5. Conduct risks assessment: determine process gaps that may permit theft, embezzlement, or fraud.
6. Review staffing, processes, and systems for assuring segregation of duties.
7. Provide for consistency in business practices: these practices in the different functions of the business serve the same purposes and goals.
8. Establish benchmarks: serve staff performance for product delivery and customer satisfaction.
9. Conduct regular review of financial performance and business value.
10. Improve productivity: review costs reduction possibilities and product delivery timetables.
11. Strengthen business transactions and reporting processes for improving informed decision-making, tax reporting, and safeguards.
12. Conduct cycle process and transactions audits to insure financial statements accuracy and integrity.

Financial institutions can ask the business for their policies and procedures as evidence of adequate internal controls before funding it. They may require such practices to be in place prior to making a loan to reduce their risks exposure. Independent audits of internal controls for a business seeking to execute an initial public offering (IPO) may notate any internal controls deficiencies and the risks they pose for shareholder investment.[5] The Securities and Exchange Commission (SEC) requires 2 or 3 years of audited financial statements depending on company size. Any material deficiencies due to a lack of policies and procedures could influence any IPO date.

Therefore, business practices are important issues for inclusion in the budget process. Over time, their rewards would be significant cost savings in liability insurance and the prevention of losses to the business due to fraud, theft, embezzlement, or other losses.

Funding Management of the Organization and Its Processes

The budget considers funding for both the organization and its processes. Without well-planned cash flow, funding the organization and processes cannot occur successfully. Pro forma cash flow acts as a benchmark for actual cash receipts and disbursements. The statement of cash flows represents decisions made for producing products and services delivered to the customer and compensation in return for them. Therefore, it is essential that the budget include a pro forma cash flow statement to measure uses and sources of funds for the budgeted year(s). Budgeting cash flow establishes the measurements for revenue, expenses, and working capital.

The budgeted cash flow will also determine additional external funding requirements, such as a loan or additional equity funding, for specific capital projects or revenue generating activities. The budget team needs to have a discussion around whether the budget requires additional funding to support increase in new customer business, projects for new market penetration, or product development.

There are several external sources for additional funding toward product, market, or channel expansion: debt funding from various financial institutions and equity funding from private investors. Financial institutions and investors are significant constituents. Their involvement in the company cannot be minimized. They must integrate into the business through stated policies and procedures that identify and foster the relationships and define their interaction.

These funding sources place a priority on business value. Company value relies on revenue generation. Management, markets, and products drive this revenue. Before financial institutions or investors consider funding through debt or private equity placement in a business, they want to know that risk factors do not exceed their parameters and that they will receive their targeted return. From this perspective, the lender or investor acts as benchmark agents for further business investments into growth and expansion. The company can measure their success according to the criteria the lender or investor sets as requirements for their funding.

Action Plan

Beginning with and examining the organization from the purpose of simplification and efficiency enables a company to eliminate activities, processes, and resources not contributing to business growth, expansion, value, and wealth.

Organizational Questionnaire and Risks Assessment

Walk through the questionnaires in Tables 6.1 and 6.3 for each component of your organization. What areas do you need to address in the budget?

1. Begin making a list of risk issues with current processes. What impact are they having on the organization in terms of prospect for losses? Identify a ballpark of resources for deriving action plans for resolving these risks. See Table 6.4 for an example of a risk exposure checklist.
2. The controller or CFO reviews the three financial statements for essential information that informs a company about its decisions. Were there pro forma financial statements prepared before the current fiscal year? How did the company perform against them?
3. Review your accounting system for adequacy and features for setting up budgets. Review the chart of accounts for being able to establish subaccounts for your budgets and reporting on them according to organizational components.

Table 6.4. Risks Exposure Identification Checklist

Risks exposure	Potential losses	Resource requirements for resolution

Preparing pro forma financial statements makes possible the measurement of business performance through targets and established benchmarks. The budgeting process enables companies to prepare reliable pro forma financial statements. These statements along with their corresponding financial ratios become business benchmarks. All three financial statements (income statement, balance sheet, and statement of cash flows) contain data on different segments of the business.

These data are essential for not only analyzing past performance but also for current and future decision-making. For example, how many months of cash does the company have to satisfy financial obligations? This is a question aimed at cash flow. What will be the loan balances at the end of the budgeted period? How much interest will be expensed during that period? These are critical budget issues associated with all three financial statements. If the business relied only on the income statement, these questions would go unanswered and could compromise the integrity of performance measurements.

During financial review of past business performance, the company gleans critical data from all three financial statements for decisions influencing business performance. Loan amortizations and balances are also business performance issues. All three statements are also essential for forecasting. Without all three, uncertainty would rest with one-third or two-thirds of the business. A company needs more than simply a portion of information for sound strategic management decisions.

CHAPTER 7

Key Management Areas

Budgeting Foundations

Business success depends on management decision-making from hindsight and insight for razor focused foresight without which careful oversight would be highly difficult at best.

Objectives

After completing this chapter, you will be able to accomplish the following toward the budget process:

1. Identify KMAs as key managerial components of your company.
2. Identify the importance of KMAs for better management of organizational components and the company's constituents.
3. Define the management chart for your company.
4. Apply KMAs for identifying key control points, risks, their funding, and how they are part of financial reporting.
5. Identify resource requirements according to each KMA in your organization: staffing, capital equipment (useful life of over 1 year), outsourcing, and supplies.

Basic Building Blocks and KMAs

Those who manage share several common characteristics. They are responsible for a portion of the organization and processes. They are accountable for their work to or for others. Some work in the business, producing and adding value. Others work on the business, designing, creating, strategizing, planning, and managing money. All of them have their roles, responsibilities, and contribute toward the company mission. The key term that describes what both sets of people do is "manage."

The other part of management is the division of labor. Such division creates efficiency and productivity. No one person can perform all the work in a company, because no one person has the talent and skills to manage every business component. The division of labor is why the modern company has a number of segments with the specializations of each segment contributing to productivity and value. People with the right skills and talent manage these segments toward the result of attaining and retaining customers and corresponding revenue and growth.

When these specialized segments of a company rise to the level of significance in their individual contribution, the company identifies their specific contribution and delegates someone to manage them. This action continues to occur for greater productivity and efficient use of resources as the company grows. Some segments are specialties relegated to a specific division of a company (such as production), while others serve the entire company (such as information technology or finance). An organizational chart is an attempt to identify organizational segments. In both cases, there is connectivity between the segments, each having its required resources for its part in product and service delivery.

The management scenario described above can present a challenge to managing financial resources for the entire company. For this purpose, this book introduces a way of bringing together significant organizational segments, their processes, and the funding for them: key management areas (KMAs). Management is the key principle for this integration. It includes such cooperative activities as planning, control (or management), and evaluation, an unending circle through which productive work occurs toward mission accomplishment.

KMAs assist the firm in addressing the management of business key organizational components for reporting on the processes that develop and provide products and services. They also offer a framework for gaining a better grip on managing the entire business organization and its constituents, such as customers, vendors, employees, investors, and financial institutions. They also raise these organization components' importance and the importance of the constituents they represent so that they do not become isolated "functions" with secondary oversight or become a lost disconnected component of the business.

The purpose of this book is to address a managerial chart to compensate for what an organizational chart often does not do with KMAs as components of organization. The organization must take into account KMAs for

1. facilitating managing the resources, processes, and funding;
2. linking the organization and processes to the financial statements for reporting their performance; and
3. managing the company's constituents who have a stake in its success.

The KMA model fulfills these objectives. KMAs are instrumental for bringing these resources together and allocating them to various tasks and duties through developed processes. This efficient resource allocation goes toward supporting overall business efforts of creating value through

1. managing markets and customers;
2. increasing revenues; and
3. maximizing profits.

For the greatest efficiency, the organization must incorporate related organizational components. These related components allow processes the shortest route (critical path) through which product and service delivery can occur with the least amount of time and expense and greatest efficiency and productivity. That is, one of the purposes of processes is to connect related activity and identify unrelated activity and resources for elimination. KMAs are common entities with most companies and industries, because everyone has products or services to offer customers— a company's primary constituent, and the reason it is in business.

The organization chart by itself does not communicate the business management model but only the organizational model. It is a static diagram showing specific divisions and reporting structures. As needed as this structure is, the managerial components receive minimal notice in terms of how they appear throughout a company. Many are even omitted, especially outsourced ones. Consequently, the organization chart is somewhat inadequate for expressing what the company really looks like, how it operates, and what the strategic links are between processes. The KMA model integrates the organizational chart with a managerial chart.

The KMAs show where management of processes and transactions occur. The organization chart is limited in this manner. KMAs manage organizations, processes, constituents, equipment, and material in constant movement toward fulfillment of mission and objectives.

One advantage of KMAs is that they focus on key constituents such as customers, vendors, bankers, investors, and employees. This focus includes not only their retention but also the evaluation of their performance or the company's performance for them.

The KMAs Model

The KMAs model illustrated in Figure 7.1 identifies how KMAs flow from the organization building block. They are key segments of business operations and their processes. Each of these KMAs consists of human,

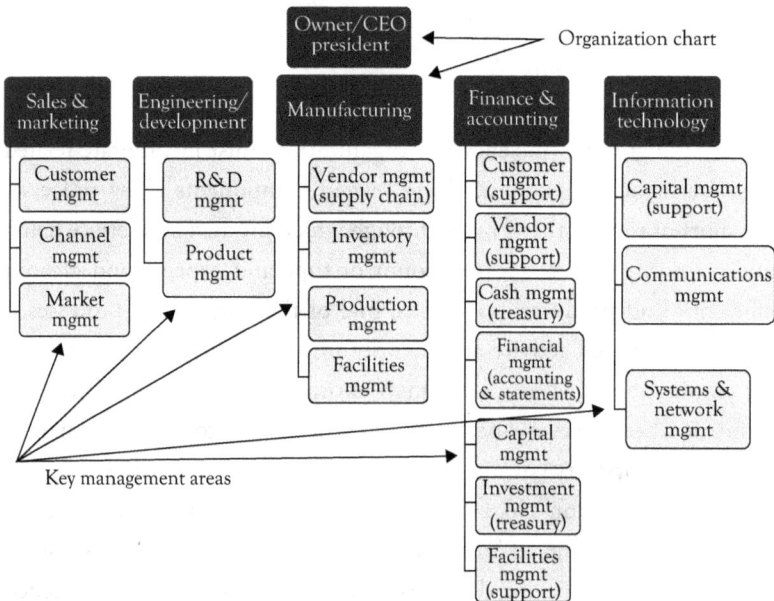

Figure 7.1. Key management areas and the company organization chart.

Note: The KMAs shown may appear more than once due to the supporting role of the organization to which it is associated.

capital, and material resources that must be budgeted, accounted for, and reported.

Not all firms have the same set of these management areas. Most professional services firms will not manufacture a product or carry inventory. Regardless if a firm has all of them or not, managing them does not change. The firm simply selects the KMAs that fit the business. Then it determines how they fit into the organization chart for the best alignment of related management components and greatest efficient use of resources toward company objectives and customer service.

Through KMAs, the business is able to focus clearly on the areas of the business it needs to manage. The KMA model has this advantage over the functional model in that it identifies business management units. This model provides clearly defined management control points for process routes through the organization. A management control point is a clearly defined area in business processes where key financial transactions occur. Rose Hightower identifies control points as "'handoffs' between processes."[1]

Although control points consist of "handoffs," they are much more than handoff components since they have economic impact and influence the financial statements. Control points in the organization and their corresponding processes incorporate:

1. Documentation of financial transactions
2. Time
3. Responsibilities
4. Performance accountability
5. Risk management

Since KMAs are higher level control points, they must receive the greatest visibility in financial and management reporting and thereby have the greatest oversight. For example, vendor management is the gateway for the supply chain. It is the major area where expense management is most critical. A number of cost control points exist within vendor management:

1. Vendor qualification and sourcing
2. Negotiated price points
3. Terms of payment
4. Purchasing

5. Lead-time

6. Receiving

7. Quality control

8. Invoicing

9. Disbursements

All of these have an influence on costs (economic activity). Unless the company views vendor management as a major component that needs greater oversight, vendor selection could be costly by perhaps not meeting critical requirements for the company or incurring greater cost. Since all of the above-listed functions relate to vendor management, this management area becomes highly instrumental in the budget process and financial reporting.

KMAs are also able to better mark out work process flow for the assignment of human, equipment, and material resources. This in turn aids in identifying budget-funding requirements.

KMAs for Better Constituent Management

When managing from a KMA model, the company organizes its business around three primary segments—its constituents, processes, and funds. Company constituents consist of vendors, customers, employees, investors, and financial institutions. A company wants to ensure that it integrates its constituents thoroughly into its business processes for supporting its success. In the event the company decides to outsource an entire business component or management area, the organization chart reflects vendors to whom the company outsources parts of its business.

For example, the Sales and Marketing organization has not only revenue and expense oversight but also development of the company's prime constituent—the customer. These two groups develop and qualify customer business, draw up customer contracts or agreements, close the sale, and mediate product or service delivery. The Finance organization plays a supporting role (invoicing and collections) in customer management, but the major portion of it resides with Sales and Marketing—a dual management oversight. The budget manager simply has to review the KMAs for which that manager has oversight for determining the relevancy of its processes toward product and service delivery and the resource and funding requirements for those processes. A company not only budgets its resources but also budgets the management of those resources. Drucker states, "Management has to give direction to the institution it manages."[2] Because it is the overall driver for productive activity, it becomes greater than the sum of its parts. It is greater because of its importance as a practice and because of the principle of leadership that flows from it. Budgeting is a management activity. For this reason, KMAs stress the management principle and incorporates the company's constituents from internal or external sources.

KMAs in Financial Reporting

The KMAs have a direct relationship with the financial statements. The balance sheet reports on liabilities incurred from vendors and subsequent disbursements to them. The income statement reports expenses incurred from vendor purchases. This direct relationship makes the KMA model one that provides greater organizational responsibility and accountability and for financial reporting. This responsibility includes planning and budgeting of revenues and expenses related to the chart of accounts and their subsequent reporting in the financial statements.

Each budget manager exercises accountability over specific accounts for budgets and performance. The income statement reflects how well each budget manager performs with funds allocated to human, equipment, and material resources. For example, as Sales and Marketing manage the customer, this determines performance and accountability for revenue. Sales and Marketing are also responsible for *customer management*, *channel management*, and *market management* and their corresponding revenue and marketing expense accounts. Each of these three KMAs plays a significant role in revenue generation. They foster the company's primary constituent, the customer, and thereby stand out as major KMAs and revenue drivers.

Channel management addresses the critical area of distribution of goods and services and involves a host of activities for ensuring that the customer receives them. It is on the other side of vendor management in the supply chain in one part of the process and is part of the supply chain in the ongoing process of product and service delivery to the customer. Channel management involves reseller or distributor selection and training or direct to customer development (vertical integration). Channel management brings about the sales activity, while marketing management focuses on presales activities. Marketing management plays just as significant a role as channel management by attracting customers to the company through promotion, pricing, packaging, and placement. Transactions and evaluation occur with all of them. Since they are major segments of the business, they qualify as KMAs.

The same holds true for the others identified on the company's managerial chart, such as Information Technology or Production. All of the supporting organizations to Sales and Marketing are cost centers. Both the selling and operational components within the business are responsibility centers for good reason. Management and responsibility work hand-in-hand. As responsibility centers, KMAs exercise "control over costs, revenues, and/or investment funds."[3]

As each organization plans its budget, the budget manager of each receives a set of accounts for identifying their expenses. Each reviews the KMAs under his or her purview for identifying the resource requirements to manage each area. When finished, Finance integrates all revenues, expenses, assets, and liabilities into the financial statements for a pro forma set of financial statements.

Allocating KMAs in Organization Management

A company can allocate KMAs in a meaningful manner to whichever organizational box it believes is most efficient and caters to the shortest route (or critical path) through the organizational structure. For example, vendor management calls upon two components of the business in a manufacturing company: that of inventory and production materials and that of accounting (cost accounting). Some manufacturing companies have the buyer logically closely aligned with MRP because of its integration in the production process. The buyer has authorization for vendor qualification, establishment of terms, materials requisition, and supplier outsourcing as needed.

However, the processes for vendor management reporting and disbursements can pose a problem in terms of safeguards unless seen as a supporting and separate role under the principle of segregation of duties.

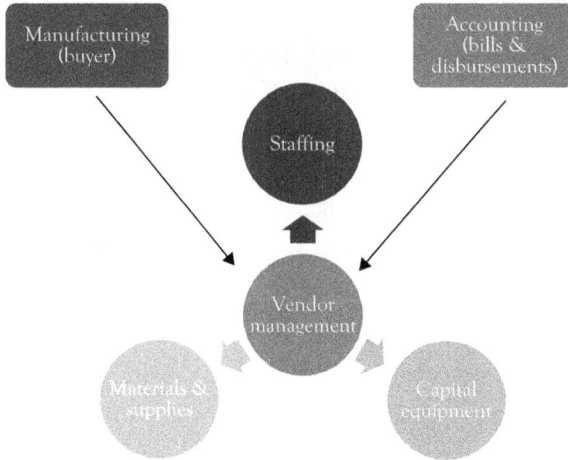

Figure 7.2. Organization and vendor KMA integration.

For this reason, Accounts Payable normally resides in Finance for better cash management and for exercising safeguards. Consequently, vendor management in reality resides in two separate organizations with dual management. In one industry (manufacturing), accounting serves in a supportive role, whereas in other industries, it is centralized altogether in Finance.

For general and administrative expenses, the accounting organization normally assumes responsibility of vendor qualification and terms. Its support for other organizational functions consists of managing vendor reporting, aging of accounts, and disbursements. Budget managers account for their oversight for their portion of vendor management in their planning for resource requirements. Figure 7.2 illustrates the dual management role over a KMA. Once organization budget managers identify resource requirements for vendor management, they can then determine the budget required for managing KMAs.

KMAs as a Strong Budgetary Control System

This brings us to two of the major financial and budgetary controls policies a company can have—budgetary responsibility and expenditure authority levels. Budgeting must include policy for exercising strong safeguards in the business. As we discovered in Chapter 5, leadership encompasses responsibility and accountability. Responsibility defines the scope of management, while accountability identifies performance oversight.

The management portion of the business is one of the most crucial management controls. As noted earlier, the company budgets management of resources as well as the resources themselves. The price paid for equipment or staff is the cost for a management decision. Consequently, every management decision has a cost. Peter Drucker states this rather adroitly:

> Management—which is the organ of society specifically charged with making resources productive, that is, with the responsibility for organized economic advance—therefore reflects the basic spirit of the modern age.[4]

Therefore, the charter of "making resources productive" represents the core control mechanism for the business in exercising safeguards over assets and directing resources toward growth or "economic advance."

Signature authority naturally integrates with management responsibility. Responsibility oversees organization and processes, while signature authority oversees company funds. These two work together as management control parts for oversight of the business environment, risks, processes, information and communications, performance evaluation, and reporting. This management oversight drives the integrity of the financial statements, the budgeting cycle, and business performance that the budget measures during the budgeted period.

Action Items

The organization chart and KMAs brings together business resources with management components. Together they manage these resources and drive the business toward success as measured by objectives and the financial numbers set forth in the budget. The KMAs model demonstrates that management is the key driver for results. Business thrives on results or it will soon cease to exist. That is the major reason for organizing business into KMAs. Without the consideration of the components of KMAs, the organization chart would be a grouping of resources without direction and clarity. Management gives it direction.

Table 7.1. KMAs Managerial Chart

KMA leader	KMA	Organization	Constituent

Constituents could not integrate well into the company structure without a framework that identifies their place like KMAs. KMAs group and link similar activities, business components, and constituents toward goal attainment. KMAs clarify all the resources of the business that contribute to gaining and retaining consequent revenues. Therefore, constituents are also business resources identified by KMAs.

KMAs facilitate processes development. Once established, the lines drawn between them give direction for the flow of work toward supplying customers with products. Their definition arrives first in the budget cycle, because they are foundational to budgeting.

Make a list of the KMAs in your business and associate them with your company's organizational chart much like the illustration in Table 7.1. Once you have the KMAs associated with the organization chart, you can identify the human, capital and material resources with each KMA. Assigning budgetary costs to these resources now becomes an easier matter. You can also easily associate constituents (suppliers, employees, investors, lenders, etc.) with them in this type of diagram. The identity of KMAs as operational performance components allows budget managers to gauge business management performance in a more meaningful manner.

STAGE II

The Pro Forma Financial Statements

CHAPTER 8

Sales Plan

The difference between selling and sold is possession and ownership.

Objectives

After completing this chapter, you will be able to accomplish the following toward the budget process:

1. Identify the budget fundamentals for sales planning.
2. Identify the difference between baseline and objective-driven budgeting and apply both in the budget process.
3. If you are using the Microsoft Excel workbook included with the purchase of this book, prepare your sales plan using the following spreadsheets in the *Business Budget Builder* Microsoft Excel workbook:

   a. Product List spreadsheet
   b. Sales Detail spreadsheet
   c. Market Expansion spreadsheet.

Foundations for a Successful Sales Forecast

This chapter addresses more than just preparing a set of sales numbers for a budget. The budget is the financial forecast and management tool for the business strategy or plan. To accommodate businesses that do not have a prepared strategic or business plan, this chapter includes sales activity checklists and guidance for the budget.

Marketing and sales can be one of the most challenging parts of a reliable budget. Market, economic, and regulatory uncertainty make it challenging. When preparing your sales forecast, consider such uncertainties.

What impact will they have on your sales? Other reasons for the challenge of sales revenue forecasting is that marketing and sales encompass the variables of market definition and segmentation, positioning, competition, channels, distribution, and even mergers and acquisition (M&A). The latter variable presents one of the greatest challenges because of the length of time an M&A may take.

Baseline and Objective-driven Budgeting

There are several ways of budget planning, and given the volatility of markets, they are more informative and educational rather than exact. Some are more analytical and quantitative, while research, markets definition, and decision-making informed by historical analysis serve as the basis for others. J. Scott Armstrong of the Wharton School of Business suggests two methods for sales forecasting:[1]

1. Extrapolation—This method works from trends rather than primarily market data. Such trends include historical data and seasonality.
2. Causal—This method relies on causal factors such as market size, company decisions, intermediaries (suppliers and distributors), competitors, market share, and external environmental factors.

The extrapolation method lends to a percentage increase based on historical trends. In such a case, marketing and economic conditions should bear heavy weight with such an analysis. If you do not combine marketing and economic conditions with your extrapolations, you could miss the mark with your sales forecasts.

The causal method of examining a number of relevant variables can increase forecast confidence. It examines influencing variables to determine how and why they contribute to sales. Using a combination of both can add to confidence because one looks to the past, while the other looks to the present and future. Both assume a baseline. Extrapolating revenue numbers from prior years is essentially working from a baseline. Causal analysis looks to the baseline and the variables underlying baseline performance. It then assesses current market and economic condition and a revenue forecast based on these and expected conditions. Both also consider the reliability of the data examined and factor that data into a set of sales numbers. However, sales numbers from these two factors may not be sufficient even though the basis for them may be reliable. Consequently, this discussion adds a third method for determining sales revenue targets—objectives.

The baseline identifies your starting point for your budget prior to setting objectives. One factor that Armstrong seems to omit is objective setting. He discusses decision-making based on forecast methodology, but decisions without targets have nothing to hit regardless if decisions include causal factors or an extrapolation from historical revenue data and market conditions. Setting market-based objectives takes you beyond the baseline, while relying on historical trends and causal market factors. Baseline planning reviews prior year revenue performance and makes projections based on trends or seasonality. However, market forces call for a more rigorous and in-depth sales forecast analysis for growth beyond current trends or a percentage of sales growth.

The baseline is important as a beginning point for budget preparation. Its neglect omits valuable information that identifies current customer base and current and future customer requirements. It also provides critical information on past performance from applied resources and informs decisions concerning resources for future performance. Two major weaknesses of baseline budgeting is that it fails to consider future market variables, economic conditions, or new initiatives. In addition, it is a passive way of making projections.

Although baseline budgeting has these two weaknesses, they do not discount its value and use. Table 8.1 provides a checklist of critical sales analysis metrics valuable for your historical analysis to determine a sales baseline. All the metrics in Table 8.1 independently provide useful but limited information. For example, sales by customer inform the company about specific customer's buying behavior (e.g., regularity, quantity, price-performance, and demand). However, the environment or conditions under which they purchased products or services may not necessarily be the same in future years. In addition, in spite of all efforts, some customers may not return in the future due to any number of variables. In addition, spikes due to one-time buyers who do not return could skew historical results.

Table 8.1. A Checklist for Establishing a Baseline from Historical Financial Data

Sales baseline checklist from historical data
1. Sales by customer
2. Sales by region or geographical segment
3. Sales by business segment and product line
4. Sales by account executive or sales manager
5. Sales by individual product
6. Top 10 customers and the ratio between these and total sales
7. Sales by contract (if you are a professional services company, such as an accounting or marketing firm, you may in addition want to examine billable of time ratios for setting sales expectations based on service billing)
8. Sales by project (if you are a building general or subcontractor, you may also wish to subdivide these sales by type of project such as residential or commercial)
9. Seasonality trends

When used together, you can distill highly informative data for making an educated baseline forecast. For example, sales by geographical area or business segment will inform you where to place emphasis during the upcoming budgeted period. In addition, if a large number of sales are overly concentrated in your top 10 customers, this concentration may be a clue about the risk the firm may be taking and opportunity elsewhere it may be missing. Therefore, before making a sales forecast based on baseline, consider all of these metrics together. They contribute to a balanced approach. Your company may also have other metrics you may wish to include.

Each of these metrics may have various levels of importance to the company. For example, sales by customer may not be as relevant or meaningful in construction or retail as it is for a printing company or accounting or legal firms. Therefore, it would assume a lower weight for measuring sales efforts. To solve the challenge of which metrics are the most to least important, assign a weight to each metric and select the top four or five. These top four or five will become the key bases for setting your objectives.

Keep in mind that a baseline simply informs you about past performance and trends and establishes parameters. As stock market analysts caution, the past is no indicator for future performance. This maxim carries significant weight in preparing a budget. Economic and market conditions swing widely from year to year and even from quarter to quarter. A sound budget is based on much more than a baseline. Determining sales projections from a baseline is a more passive approach but an important starting point. Preparing revenue objectives is more proactive.

Baseline budgeting could also ignore a number of external assumptions such as the economy, industry, buying behavior, and markets, variables that swing widely during the budget period. For example, assume your sales manager projects a 30%–40% increase in sales. What are your bases of estimate? Would you reach that increase from existing base resources alone? Do your sales forecast numbers rely on increases over prior year when the economy may have been rather explosive or anemic? Would it also be realistic to assume such an increase with current resources or simply a corresponding percentage increase in supporting resources? That is, would you simply increase hiring and other operating expenses in relation to or a percentage of your sales forecast? In the latter case, if sales came in significantly lower than expected, this could have a material impact on the bottom line if the company increased resources to handle the expected sales that did not materialize.

Trends analyses provide insight into decisions along a timeline, especially if the firm has 2–3 years of financial data to review. It identifies spikes in sales due to one-time sales variables and other revenue fluctuations. However, trends analyses is also limited and a passive way of arriving at a sound sales forecast.

Setting Sales Objectives

Sales objectives take into account your revenue streams such as channels, distribution, alliances, affiliates, partnerships, and joint ventures. If you kept track of these segments in terms of unit sales on a period basis, you have an advantage in setting objectives for them and in measuring their successes and shortcomings.

Prior to establishing objectives for the budget period, consider their contribution to your revenue stream over past periods in terms of the BCG matrix shown in Figure 8.1. The BCG matrix originated with the Boston Consulting Group (BCG) for examining product life cycle. It has shown to have decision-making value for determining strengths

BCG matrix

	Question marks	Stars
High	Question marks	Stars
	Remainder divested ← Select a few →	
	Low market share and high market growth	**High market share and high market growth**
	The opportunities no one knows what to do with. These opportunities need serious thought as to whether increased investment is warranted.	You're well-established, and these are fantastic opportunities
		Invest
	Dogs ← Liquidate	**Cash cows**
	Low market share and Low market growth	**High market share and Low market growth**
	Your market presence is weak. It's going to be difficult to make a profit.	You're well-established. However, the market isn't growing and your opportunities are limited.
Low		

Market growth (vertical axis, Low to High)

Low ◄ Market share ► High

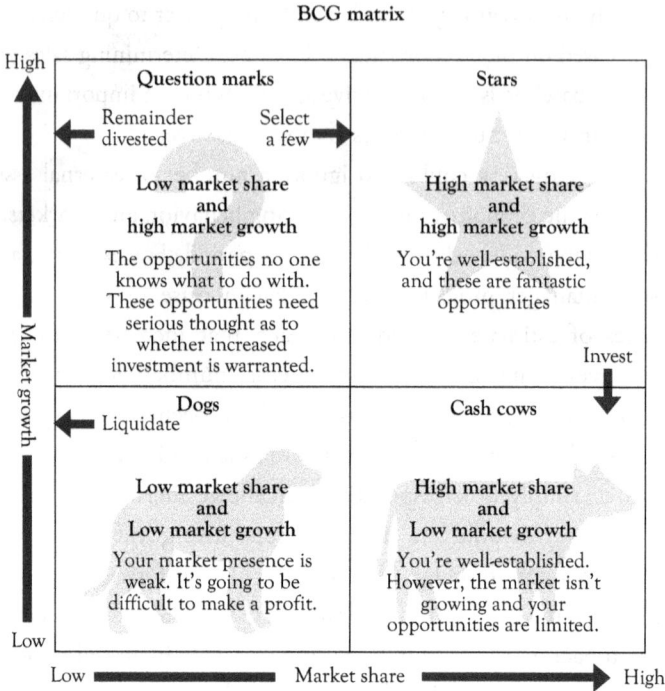

Figure 8.1. BCG matrix for sales forecasting.

and weaknesses in markets for existing products. The four segments of the matrix express product strength in two dimensions: market growth and market share. Star products represent optimum growth and share, while Cash Cows represent low growth and high share. Dogs reveal weak product growth and share, while the Question Mark products identify high growth but low share or market penetration.

The value of this matrix is that you can also apply it to a number of scenarios. One such scenario is revenue stream. For example, you may have several alliances, affiliates, and partnerships, a situation highly popular in today's market arrangements. Simply substitute your products or product lines with these channels or distribution mechanisms and apply the same principles from the original BCG matrix by identifying which belong in each segment of the matrix. This arrangement can provide you with information on concentration of sales and decisions on effectiveness of your channels or distribution activity. The next step is preparing objectives based on the information gleaned from your examination whether you

Table 8.2. Revenue Objectives Matrix

Revenue stream (channel, ventures, affiliates, etc.)	Share of your business (%)	Prior years actuals 20xx to 20xx	Revenue objective	Justification

use the matrix for products, channel marketing, distribution, or geographic segments. Consider revenue objectives according to the revenue streams shown in Table 8.2. Justification for the objective could be market or economic condition, new initiatives or business, or new opportunity with a revenue stream.

Once you analyze your channels or other means of sales, the next step is setting objectives for unit sales. Unit sales differ widely among industries. In the building industry, pricing for the finished product will vary from customer to customer, because it could depend on providing a quotation for the product. This could make it more challenging for any level of budgeted sales precision. However, such a challenge is not insurmountable. Setting sales targets provide a strong alternative. The easy and more passive method for such an industry is to review past quotes and project budgeted revenue. This could lead to hiring additional staff based on increasing the sales number by a certain percentage. This technique assumes that the additional resources can generate the desired revenue.

This method bypasses setting objectives—a more proactive approach. Such objectives come before assuming more resources for creating greater sales. Hiring more staff or purchasing more equipment without first determining what you want to accomplish could increase costs without a corresponding increase in revenues and place pressure on cash flow. Rather, the objectives come first followed by identifying the resources for accomplishing them.

The following nine steps serve as an example of how to go about preparing a sales forecast for any industry in which units of production may be difficult to determine. Production in this sense does not necessarily refer to a manufacturing environment. In this sense, production refers to a deliverable to customers whether they are hard products or services.

1. Identify the number of productive units delivered to the customer associated with a price (e.g., a home, remodel, or related types of construction for delivery to customers).
2. Determine pricing based on prior experience or market pricing for such units or whatever price you set for the unit.
3. Identify the market locations, channels, or distribution sources you want to target.
4. Prepare a market plan to reach customers in those specific targeted markets.
5. Identify partners or others with whom to work (a general contractor) if this is part of your strategy.
6. Prepare an execution strategy for implementing your marketing plan.
7. Develop a full sales revenue forecast based on completion and delivery of all units.
8. Hire or purchase the required resources for meeting your targeted units for each type of product (home or remodel).
9. Track progress against targeted units and price points for each unit.

These nine steps can work with any product or service divisible by units (e.g., hours or pay-per-click). Companies in similar industries that prepare job or project quotations can also take advantage of this sales model.

Action Items

The following actions can prove to be useful in working through your marketing and sales plan.

1. If you have been in business a number of years, review your historical results according to the checklist in Table 8.1, "A Checklist for

Establishing a Baseline from Historical Financial Data." Consider the following questions:

 a. What are your revenue expectations for current customers?
 b. What are your prospects for new customers or clients?
 c. What regional or geographical sales trends do you see? What does this tell you about future prospects?
 d. Are your products or services divided into product lines? Which have the best showings? Which ones have the poorest showing? What do your individual products tell you about their sales performance?
 e. Review other items in Table 8.2 for establishing a baseline for total sales. The ones in Table 8.2 are among the most common among businesses.

2. Are you introducing new products in the budget period? When? Is your market plan realistic? Read the section "Components of Objectives" in Chapter 4 for the process of preparing objectives. Your sales projections will drive production capacity, inventory levels, processes management, and resources acquisition.

3. Now is the time to prepare your sales plan. If you are using the Microsoft Excel *Business Budget Builder*, complete the following spreadsheets:

 a. Product List
 b. Sales Detail
 c. Market Expansion.

Read the instructions for each spreadsheet before starting.

CHAPTER 9

Capital Plan

It takes capital to produce wealth and wealth progress and progress a civilization

Objectives

After completing this chapter, you will be able to accomplish the following toward the budget process:

1. Perform a capital plan assessment by examining your organizational and processes for identifying capital requirements.
2. Develop a comprehensive capital plan for your entire company.
3. If you are using the Microsoft Excel workbook included with the purchase of this book, prepare your capital plan using the Capital Budget spreadsheet. Select menu item 10 in the Getting Started spreadsheet.
4. Use evaluation methods (menu item 11) in the *Business Budget Builder* Microsoft Excel workbook for evaluating and selecting capital projects.

Capital Plan Assessment

The capital plan is sufficiently important to address independent of the balance sheet because it could encompass a sizable investment for supporting market strategies and objectives. The capital plan has a significant impact on all three financial statements. It influences tax planning, business net worth and value, funding decisions, and cash flow. The capital plan encompasses the following:

1. Market opportunities review for supporting capital resource requirements
2. Identification of replacement costs

3. Impact on the income statement for tax purposes
4. Cash flow
5. Evaluation of prospective capital decisions
6. A calendar to place new assets in service

Market Opportunity Review

The capital plan begins with marketing and sales. Once you settle on marketing opportunities from the view of existing and new products, expansion, or channels, the budgeting team collaborates on plant and equipment purchases necessary to support opportunity efforts. It also determines capital purchases for the supporting KMAs. Several questions arise concerning capital requirements for your company:

- Can you reach projected sales without additional capital purchases?
- Will existing equipment be sufficient to support sales efforts?
- What increase in sales or cost savings would the new equipment generate?

Capital Assets Assessment and Purchase Calendar Plan

The capital plan has four parts to it:

1. Existing assets and their current useful life
2. New assets and their classification and useful life
3. Disposal of assets during the budget period
4. Evaluating capital asset purchases

After finalizing the sales plan, the company turns to the resources for supporting it. Among the most significant categories of resources are capital assets. Each organization must first consider if existing capital assets are sufficient for that organization to support the sales revenue plan. Part of that consideration rests with the adequacy of existing capital assets. If some assets cannot meet the requirements for supporting the sales plan, then consider their retirement or removal from service. Common means of retiring them from service is selling them or scraping for salvage value.

Quite frequently, many businesses omit this activity from the budget plan when planning for new capital equipment. Its omission could lead to surprising substantial budget variances if the dollar amount of capital equipment retirement and disposal is considerable, such as large production machines or vehicles. Such an omission can negatively affect net income.

The same holds true for discontinued operations such as plant closures. If a company does not consider plant closure in the budget, it can take a substantial hit to net income. While this book is not one on accounting principles, it remains important to consider discontinued operations in the budget if a firm anticipates such an event at the start of the budget cycle. Check with your CPA or CFO during the budget process for the application of accounting rules related to discontinued operations for ensuring that you budget accordingly.

The next step in the capital plan is for acquisition of new capital equipment. Capital expenditures consider several variables for preparing the capital plan for the budget period:

1. Capital requirements for supporting the sales plan
2. Timeframe for capital outlays within the budgeted period
3. Placement in service for depreciation purposes (this could be a different date than the actual purchase date, especially when considering capital equipment installation)
4. Whether to classify any financed equipment as capital lease or operating lease
5. The return on investment for equipment purchases (e.g., cost savings or revenue generation)
6. Financing requirements, including cost of money, if the entire capital budget cannot be financed internally
7. How and where the equipment will be used
8. The classification of equipment for booking purposes
9. The identification of recovery periods and elected Section 179 or bonus depreciation (check the most recent laws, which change yearly)
10. Whether the planned purchased equipment will be new or used (this will have a bearing on depreciation allowance as well as selection evaluation)

A number of the items in the above checklist are under the purview of the CFO or company CPA. The above items have tax implications and for consideration in the budget for not incurring variances during the budget period or year.

Specific Areas for Capital Plan Evaluation

When taking your capital plan into account, consider the following major categories:

1. Financial Management Applications—If your accounting system does not track transactions to accommodate the above analysis or is not set up to do so, you may wish to address whether to move to another accounting application or use third party applications. Since budgeting is the primary financial management and internal financial control practice for the business, it touches on all business resources requirements.

2. Information Technology Requirements for Customer Efforts and Business Support—Information technology (IT) equipment requirements is a necessary analysis for critical safeguard over company information. Consider internal controls for deciding on existing, used, or new equipment and any upgrades in hardware and software applications. This is important for entire company security interaction with constituents such as vendors, customers, and employees. Do your employees telecommute and require remote access? Do suppliers need access for inventory stocking purposes? Do you need communications with customers, such as through an FTP site or related mechanisms? Do you maintain IT internally or outsource it? If the answer is yes to any of these questions, then remote access and security protocols are vital for protection against infiltration, viruses, malware, spyware, and related risks to your company.

   To insure that you address all IT systems issues, conduct an assessment in the following way:

   a. Develop an IT requirements checklist.
   b. Identify your current setup.

c. Determine gaps in your IT system and its management.

d. Identify requirements for dealing with these gaps.

e. Perform an IT systems costs analysis including implementation.

f. Prepare the capital budget for it.

Security is only one of several criteria for IT requirements and management. Sagacent Technologies, Inc. offers a comprehensive checklist useful for making an evaluation. Those items include some of the following:[1]

a. Technology management

b. Managed services and remote support (for outsourced IT)

c. Infrastructure and its support

d. Help desk (if outsourced)

e. Data protection and backup

f. Remote connectivity and mobility

g. Business continuity and disaster recovery

h. Server and desktop virtualization (virtual servers and desktop monitoring from a single location)

i. Audits and assessment

j. Security

k. Hosting, Internet, and Cloud services

3. Manufacturing and Production Requirements Planning— Manufacturing production and MRP efficiency and inventory accuracy depend on hardware and software applications that have all the necessary features for production, inventory, and vendor management. A best practice approach for requirements is to create a checklist of hardware and software items for features for these category requirements. Review Chapter 10, "Production Plan," to ensure that your capital plan coincides with your production plan.

4. Marketing and Sales Equipment—Consider the events and campaigns you plan during the budget period or year for capital outlays. In addition to computers and related equipment, do you plan trade shows or conferences? Then consider the capitalization of booth displays and similar assets.

5. Internal Operations versus Outsourcing—Which provides your company greater cost effectiveness: internal management or outsourcing? If outsourcing, review Appendix C, "Major Vendor Management Best Practices and Policies," for guidance on outsourcing practices and contractual arrangements.

6. Research and Development Requirements—For research and development capital requirements, review Chapter 10, "Production Plan," specifically for any facilities layout plan you developed for research and development. See Figure 9.1 as an example of a capital planning roll-up. This example is the application used in the *Business Budget Builder* Microsoft Excel workbook.

7. Asset Purchase Calendar—Purchases need to be spread over the budgeted fiscal period as their implementation and use requires. Finance then allocates the costs and related depreciation and amortization expenses accordingly for when they will be placed in service.

Capital Budgeting Evaluation Techniques

How do you know which capital acquisition plan would be most cost effective? How can you determine if purchasing new equipment is more cost effective? Will you generate a greater revenue stream than retaining current equipment, purchasing used equipment, or engaging in a lease? There are several methods available for making such decisions. This discussion focuses on four of the more frequently used ones for evaluating an investment:[2]

1. Payback or recovery (recoup) method
2. Discounted payback period
3. Accounting rate of return (ARR)
4. Net present value (NPV)

Review the Capital Equipment Evaluation spreadsheet in the *Business Budget Builder* Microsoft Excel workbook. The payback method is a simple way of evaluating different project investments. It answers

Total assets through 2013	Total assets through 2014	Accumulated depreciation Through 2014
$ 1,227,000	$ 1,356,000	$ 301,800

Total 2014 annual depreciation	Total 2014 montly depreciation
$ 68,038	$ 5,670

Assumes straight line method for budgeting purposes

CAPITAL BUDGET WORKSHEET INSTRUCTIONS

In the table below, beginning at row A18, enter the following:

A. Asset Class—The asset class defined by the Internal Revenue Code (To be Completed by your Finaance group).

B. Description—Current or description of asset (i.e., computer, printer, copier)
For all current assets, enter all assets by Asset Class on one line for each year paced in service.
For example, Current Machinery and Equipment for "Placed in service" period 2002, 2003 and so on.

C. Purchase Price—For current, enter the total dollar amount for each Asset Class.
For each new asset, enter its purchase Price.

D. Placed in Service—Enter the year asset placed in service.

E. Enter any Section 179 or Bonus deprication taken.

Assets class	Cost basis	Depr/amort
Machinery and Equipment	$ 235,000	$ 45,500
Furniture, Fixtures, Cellular Phones	80,000	13,500
Autos	56,000	52,000
Buildings	500,000	125,000
Land	125,000	—
Organizational and Startup Costs	12,500	10,000
Goodwill	45,000	32,000
Computers	15,000	7,500
Software	3,500	2,300

Assets class	Description	Purchase price	Cost basis	Placed in service	Recovery period	Section 179/bonus	Accumulated depreciation	Balance	2014 annual	2014 monthly
Machinery and Equipment	Current	250,000	235,000	2002	7	15,000	45,500	189,500	27,071	2,256
Furniture, Fixtures, Cellular Phones	Current	100,000	80,000	2002	7	20,000	13,500	66,500	9,500	792
Autos	Current	56,000	56,000	2002	5		52,000	4,000	800	67
Buildings	Current	500.00	500.00	2002	15		125,000	375,000	25,000	2,083
Land	Current	125,000	125,000	2002	0			125,000	–	–
Leasehold Improvement	Current	55,000	55,000	2002	15		13,5000	41,500	2,767	231
Organizational and Startup Costs	Current	12,500	12,5000	2002	15		10,000	2,500	167	14
Goodwill	Current	45,000	45,000	2002	15		32,500	12,500	833	69

Figure 9.1. Capital plan roll-up (see Microsoft Excel Business Budget Builder).

Table 9.1. Payback Evaluation Method

New equipment purchase	Used equipment purchase
Investment = $15,000	Investment = $10,000
Cash savings or revenue generation = $3,500	Cash savings or revenue generation = $2,000
Payback Period = 4.3 years	Payback Period = 5.0 years

the question, "What is the length of time for recovering the amount invested? This method asks for some assumptions about the investment: (1) the total cost or outlays for it and (2) the revenue or cost savings it will generate. Assume you want to determine which decision will give a shorter payback: (1) purchasing new equipment, or (2) purchasing used equipment. The illustration in Table 9.1 will provide the answer.

From this analysis, a new equipment purchase would have the shortest payback. However, this method does not take into account the time value of money or the continuation of revenue or cost savings after the payback period for determining total profitability of the investment. To account for the time value of money, use the discounted payback period. For profitability, use the ARR.

For the *discounted payback period*, you will need one other function— the discount rate, which is either the cost of capital or required rate of return. Assume the following for a capital investment:

1. Investment cost = $500,000
2. Expected revenue or cost savings = $80,000
3. Discount rate = 5%

Table 9.2 shows the results of calculating the *discounted payback period*. Perform the same calculation for any other competing investment to determine which would be the preferred capital investment.

Accounting Rate of Return

Assume the equipment has a life expectancy of 10 years (not the same as accounting useful life for depreciation purposes). Assume also that the average savings or revenue was the $80,000 per year as shown in Table 9.2,

Table 9.2. Discounted Payback Period

Years	Cash flow (500,000)	Present value factor 1.0000	Discounted cash flow (500,000)	Cumulative discounted cash flow (500,000)	
1	80,000	0.9524	76,190	(423,810)	Discount 5%
2	80,000	0.9070	72,562	(351,247)	
3	80,000	0.8638	69,107	(282,140)	
4	80,000	0.8227	65,816	(216,324)	
5	80,000	0.7835	62,682	(153,642)	
6	80,000	0.7462	59,697	(93,945)	
7	80,000	0.7107	56,855	(37,090)	
8	80,000	0.6768	54,147	17,057	
Discounted Payback Period = 7.3 yr					

Table 9.3. Accounting Rate of Return

Assumptions	
Investment	$ 500,000
Useful Life	7
Income or savings	640,000
Depreciation (Straightline)	71,429
Sales or scrap value	50,000
Calculation	
Investment Amount	$ 500,000
Total Depreciation and Disposal	121,429
Annual Rate of Return	3.5%
Formula	
[(Total Depreciation & Disposal/Investment Amount)/7]	

its annual savings or profitability rate appear in Table 9.3. If your targeted desired return is 5%, this investment would be rejected.

Investment Decisions Using NPV

The NPV considers the time value of money for a specific capital investment. That is, how much is future cash flows worth today minus the initial investment? The method in Table 9.4 will provide that answer. Like the other methods, NPV begins with certain assumptions: investment outlays and a target rate of return for discounting the net cash flows.

Table 9.4. Net Present Value Calculation

Annual NPV	
Investment Amount	500,000
Cash Flow per Period	80,000
Number of Periods	10
Discounted Rate Per Period	5.0%
Estimated Life of Investment	10
Calculations	
Investment Amount	(500,000)
Period	NPV
1	76,190
2	72,562
3	69,107
4	65,816
5	62,682
6	59,697
7	56,855
8	54,147
9	51,569
10	49,113
Total	117,739
Return	24%
Formula	
Investment Amount/(1+Discount Rate)*Period Squared(1...2...3...4)	

CHAPTER 10

Production Plan

Plan before production; it delivers.

Objectives

After completing this chapter, you will be able to accomplish the following toward the budget process:

1. Review production organization and processes for determining their related budget expenses.
2. Identify expenses related to internal controls, safeguards, and their management.
3. Develop a facilities and processes flow layout diagram for determining expenses associated with items in the diagram.
4. Prepare comprehensive facilities expense and capital budget schedules.

Production Planning

Production primarily comprises all business components that contribute directly to producing products or services for customers. Direct labor, capital (fixed assets), direct materials, and supplies are the major costs. The organizational components that occur within these industries include

- direct labor;
- direct materials;
- manufacturing and production facilities layout;
- warehousing for inventory and distribution;
- machinery maintenance and installation; and
- office space for production support (e.g., buyers, schedulers, and inventory management)

Management organizational and processes (review Chapters 4–6, 8)		
Assumptions, objectives, risks, reporting, performance	Key management areas	Resources and processes

Management practices (review Chapter 7)	
Internal controls	Control points, hand-offs

Management resource requirements
Staffing, facilities,capital, tools, materials (direct and indirect), supplies, insurance coverage

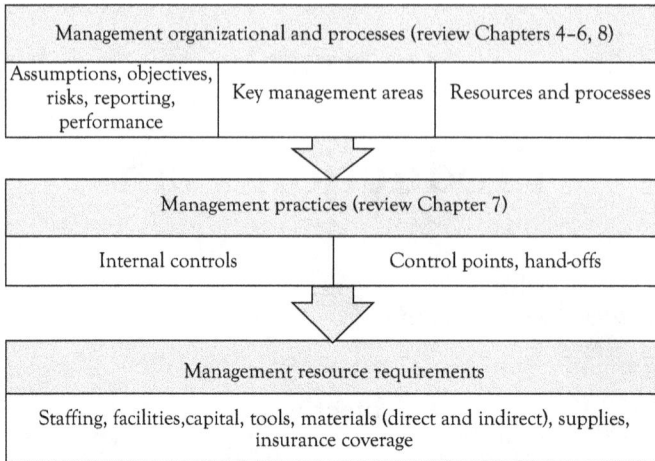

Figure 10.1. Production planning three-step process.

The production and staffing plan are interrelated and should be prepared together. The production budget is the overall plan for manufacturing. As you work through your production plan, consult Chapter 12 for preparing the staffing plan. Staffing is an integrated part of resource requirements. Working through the production budget plan helps you to identify staffing, equipment, materials, and supplies for supporting production and shipments.

The sections that follow helps lay the foundation for staffing and other resource requirements. Identify work requirements for supporting sales prior to staffing the production organization and processes. As you work through work requirements, issues may arise that would lend to modifying staffing requirements. These sections include (see Figure 10.1 "Production Planning Three-step Process"):

1. Management organizational and processes essentials
2. Management practices
3. Management resource requirements

In addition to product labor and materials, production includes production support requirements that consist of

1. MRP;
2. inventory management (receiving, stores, kitting, adjustments, cycle counting, physical inventory);

3. change control;

4. document control;

5. purchasing;

6. manufacturing packaging and engineering;

7. standards;

8. quality assurance and test;

9. shipping and receiving;

10. IT support;

11. facilities security;

12. facilities and equipment repairs and maintenance.

The following sections discuss the process for determining these resources requirements for the above.

Management Organizational and Processes Essentials

The production process has greater complexity than most other organizations within the company. Consequently, having a basis for budgeting resource requirements is a starting point. For planning resources, first consider developing a layout diagram like the one shown in Figure 10.2 Once you have identified the organizational components of the production cycle, their processes become easier to lay into the organizational plan. The production processes consist of a number of KMAs that enable you to recognize constituent involvement, especially employees, vendors, and customers. Among those KMAs are the following:

1. Production management

2. Equipment management

3. MRP management

4. Facilities management

5. Inventory management

6. Workflow (routing) management

7. Vendor management

Equipment maintenance, calibration, repairs, and updates are management tasks that require oversight. Equipment is also a resource for product development. This distinction is important for budgeting purposes for postpurchase equipment repair, warranties, and maintenance expenses. To neglect equipment, management could omit the necessary staffing and other resources for it.

Consider using the diagram in Figure 10.1, "Production Planning Three-step Process," and consult the suggested chapters. The cited chapters, along with the below sections, the first three steps, act as instructional guides for completing each step. They provide the basis for the final step of creating the production budget.

Organization and Processes

Working through and defining organizational and process requirements aid you in defining the three major budget cost factors:

1. Risks exposure
2. Information systems
3. Production and reporting

Review the organizational and processes reviews (Chapters 5 and 6) you conducted during the preplanning stage for highlighting any costs issues related to them. After reviewing them, you may discover the need to address the checklist in Table 10.1 for budgetary purposes. Table 10.1 identifies organizational or process expense drivers for production.

It is useful to make a distinction in processes between internal and outsourced operations. Internal controls are top priority for processes, and they apply to outsourced ones as well as internal processes. As necessary as they are, outsourced operations make your company more vulnerable to risks. For this reason, establishing and budgeting for management controls for outsourced operations also become a necessity.

Consult Table C.1 in Appendix C for guidelines in developing safeguards for outsourced operations. The trend in manufacturing outsourcing, especially to other countries, highlights the need to exercise greater management over production and shipments. The 16 items in Table C.1 will enable you to budget for the necessary safeguards for outsourced activity. As you consider outsourcing in the preparation of this step, you will find it helpful to read all of Appendix C.

Table 10.1. Organizational and Process Management Expense Drivers

Organizational and process management expense drivers
1. Training existing and new staff in new processes and equipment handling, management, and business processes. Do you need to bring in a trainer for these purposes or would this be a permanent internal resource?
2. Creating or updating procedures for guiding staff, safeguarding assets, manufacturing routing, and providing risks management (particularly inventories). Would you need a vendor for this project or would you hire an internal resource?
3. Equipment or software applications (primary or third party) for updating or implementing time management and collection and data processing tools to account for labor, material, and other costs for accurate reporting on production activity.
4. Defining segregation of duties for proper safeguards over confidential and proprietary data, product information, equipment management and security, and access controls. If this were needed, would you need a consultant for this project?
5. Equipment, software, staffing, or outsourced expertise for updating security and security systems for the prevention of fraud, theft, embezzlement, and other losses (e.g., the security of inventories, manufacturing data, and equipment security).
6. Production equipment or software applications for increased efficiency, scheduling (material requirements planning), planning, product delivery, and communications with your organizational team and constituents (specifically your customers and vendors).
7. Product, administrative, and facilities related outsourcing decisions (both contract and subcontract sourcing). This could be a cost-saving project depending on performing a cost-benefit analysis of performing specific functions internally.

KMAs and Management Practices

Chapter 7 highlights that KMAs are management components where greater visibility of process flow occurs for the assignment of staffing, capital, and materials. They also focus more sharply on constituents, such as customers, employees, and vendors, and their management and integration in the business. This focus applies primarily to critical high cost organizational components like outsourced payroll, IT, call centers, warehousing, product shipment, and manufacturing processes.

Frequently, it is more cost effective to use outside vendors for these activities. Consequently, contractual arrangements for vendor performance accountability become paramount. Since the trend toward outsourced production has become a much more prominent occurrence, this raises the importance of outsourced organizations to a much higher alertness and priority. This is especially true concerning interstate and offshore activities where risk management becomes a major factor. Therefore, focusing on outsourced components allows managers to be more keenly

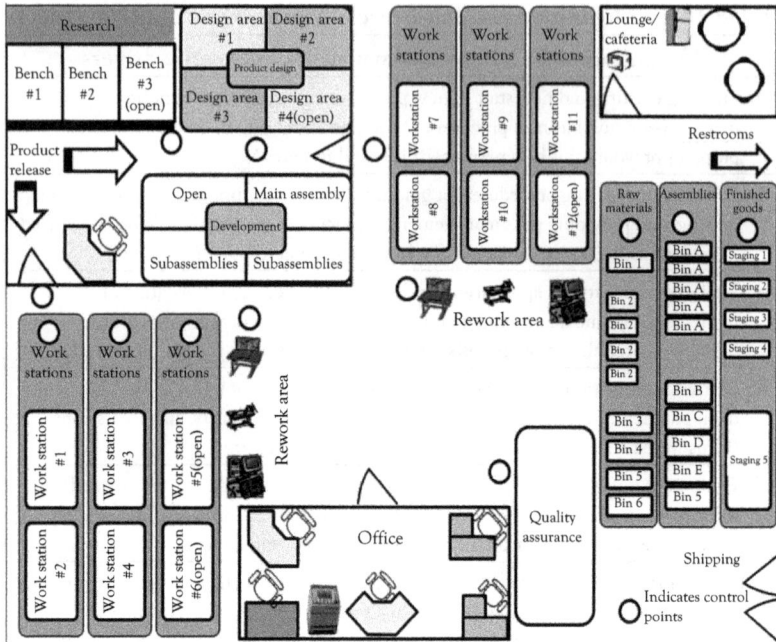

Figure 10.2. Sample production layout design.

Note: Complete a production layout for each building or production area. Control Points indicate where important documented or financial transactions occur that need reporting and tracking.

aware of the performance of resources, safeguards over transactions that occur with them, and best practices for processes. Consequently, the costs for such management cannot be ignored in the budget. When identifying objectives for outsourcing, be sure to account for the following in identifying expenses related to that objective:

1. Include internal activities related to outsourced organizational components.
2. Identify resources for managing the outsourced components (setting up its management as a project enables you to better identify internal human, equipment, and material resources for it).
3. Identify internal reporting structure for it on the organization chart and notate it as outsourced.
4. Prepare a budget for it as you would any other organizational component (e.g., total costs for the vendor contract as well as resources for managing the contract).

Facilities and Processes Flow Layout Design

This section is applicable if you do not outsource manufacturing production. Even if you do outsource a major portion of your production, this means that you maintain some of it internally. Therefore, it is a good practice to show how outsourced components interact with internal operations for being able to budget both.

A production layout diagram not only accomplishes the purpose of showing clear and efficient processes but also overlays internal controls and control points for product and asset accountability and safeguards. Such a design layout pinpoints staffing and equipment capital requirements. Once you have identified capital assets and their location in the diagram, you can tag and record them in your accounting system (if the accounting system provides for that).

Creating a facilities layout schematic for determining requirements in each management area makes your budget task easier. Figure 10.2 provides a sample layout design that gives a visual of current and expected resource requirements. In the design, you want to distinguish between existing staffing and capital and newly budgeted staffing and capital.

Your production layout would reflect both existing and prospective staff. If your staffing plan changes after completing the production layout design, ensure that you update the staffing plan to align with the staffing requirements shown on your layout design.

What remains is to identify capital, small equipment, and furnishing requirements for your layout design. Capital also includes necessary tenant or capital build-out improvements for satisfying production and workflow requirements. Capital equipment, facility improvements, furniture, jigs, and fixtures that have a useful life of over one year are included in your capital plan.

Classify all other equipment, small tools, dyes, plates, molds, or related manufacturing equipment with a useful life of less than one year as expensed items and budget them to the appropriate budget expense account associated with the income statement. Performing your production layout design in tandem with your internal controls and control points alignment will ensure that both are complete and that you identify all related expenses and capital to production.

Quantifying Resources and Their Costs

The three previous steps serve as the basis for deriving production facilities' budgeted expenses. This excludes direct material costs, which is a function of direct material bill of material requirements. You are now prepared to identify resource requirements (staffing, capital, tools, materials, supplies, and services) for expense and capital costs.

This step involves the following:

1. Organizational and Processes Management Expense Drivers—Review Table 10.1 in this chapter to determine expenses associated with staff training, procedural guideline updates, safeguards and internal controls, security, or outsourcing cost or cost-saving decisions.
2. Facilities and Processes Flow Layout Design—Review your production facilities layout to determine staffing, capital equipment, materials, or supplies expenses.
3. If you use the Microsoft Excel workbook included in the purchase of the book, enter capital equipment related to your production layout in the Capital Budget spreadsheet of the *Business Budget Builder* Microsoft Excel workbook.

CHAPTER 11

Administrative Plan

Behind every technical success is well-developed administration.

The administrative plan encompasses all indirect activities in support of sales revenue efforts. In other words, all of the expenses related to the administration of the business are classified on the income statement as sales and general and administrative expenses. It is not the purpose of this chapter to examine every line item of general and administrative expenses but to highlight some issues significant to budget items.

Attempting to correlate every single expense to sales or the production of products or services is time-consuming and unnecessary. Such a practice can be a management headache. It is much more useful to address larger expense items and their management since they have a more significant influence on budget variances and net income. Minor expenses such as supplies, bank fees, dues and subscriptions, postage, and related items can be forecasted based on a mix of historical data, a percentage adjustment, or even as a lump sum. In the latter case, budget managers identify their administrative funding requirements for minor expenses like supplies and small equipment items. They can then spread these expenses across monthly periods according to their requirements. Under this arrangement, there would be exceptions for larger expense items such as in the checklist below:

1. Capitalized items captured in the capital plan
2. Staffing and headcount prepared under the staffing plan
3. Sales commissions
4. Market research and development
5. Conferences, trade shows, and similar events and their corresponding expenses
6. Advertising and marketing expenses

7. Telecommunications
8. Equipment leases
9. Automobile allowances or expenses
10. Facility leases
11. Noncapitalized repairs and maintenance
12. Insurance requirements for one-time events if such events are not already covered under existing policies
13. Outsourced accounting, legal, and similar professional services (agents and agencies, call centers, outbound/inbound selling)

The above items receive treatment in the discussions that follow. While the elements of the operating budget have shared responsibility among the several organizations within the company, the Finance group naturally has the major responsibility over the financial budget (balance sheet and cash flow) because of its position over financial management, planning, internal controls, analysis, and reporting. Consequently, Finance's oversight extends to all balance sheet items: assets, short- and long-term liabilities, and equity. This includes contractual obligations associated with balance sheet line items.

Requirements for Supporting Customer Efforts

The key driver for indirect administrative expenses for most companies is marketing and sales. Below are some questions for each budget manager to consider related to the budget:

1. How do your costs support marketing and sales effort?
2. Does your staffing plan sufficiently support required activity for budgeted product and service delivery, warranty efforts, and customer support? Such support is not only direct but also indirect and includes any area when your company interacts with the customer for any reason including the following:

    a. Sales support
    b. Technical and warranty support
    c. Shipping and delivery

   d. Quality assurance

   e. Finance and accounting

   f. Information technology

3. Does your capital budget lend to greater productivity or cost reduction?

Supporting Expenses for the Sales and Marketing Plan

The sales and marketing organizations prepare two budgets—one for revenue and one for expenses to support that revenue. This chapter discusses sales, marketing, and administrative together because they fall in the category of operating expenses. In financial reporting, all these expenses receive treatment as selling, general, and administrative (SG&A). The sales plan discusses revenue separately.

A sales plan would be incomplete unless it considered the necessary resources for sales efforts. These budgeted expenses do not spread evenly across monthly periods. Rather, such expenses are taken into consideration when certain advanced major events payments are required and when these major events actually occur. For example, show management companies need to know the number of participants for reserving show booth space for a given marketing trade show or convention. Reservations for booth space, sponsorships, and seminar speakers normally require reservation prepayments or deposits 4–9 months in advance. Finance normally classifies prepayments to the balance sheet and reclassifies them in the months when the expenses occur. The same holds true for designing and printing collateral, retaining an agency for company branding, promotions, partnerships, joint ventures, and advertising. Therefore, when budgeting these expenses, take into consideration when these expenses will be realized.

Sales also include such planned expenses such as sales support, customer relations, and outbound and inbound sales efforts. Would you require a call center or similar type services for telesales, appointment setting, or direct response marketing? These events could necessitate expenses for vendor retention, travel, materials, and supplies expenses related to vendor efforts.

Trade Shows and Other Marketing Events

What opportunities exist from trade shows and similar marketing events for realizing sales objectives? Reviewing expenses from prior years can provide you with how well you performed in terms of return on sales and marketing expenses. A traditional method of identifying sales and marketing expenses as a percentage of sales may not be an accurate indicator of performance. This is especially true if you are a startup company with little financial accounting history on which to rely. In addition, the historical review method only reflects how much you actually spent for producing sales in prior years. Even then, they do not reflect a reality, because there are a number of variables that enter into sales performance.

A better indicator of sales performance is a sales multiple. Sales and marketing promotional expenses, for the most part, drive sales. They are the primary means of market exposure and customer attraction. Therefore, comparing how much total sales and marketing expenses multiplied sales would provide a more accurate indicator of sales performance than a percentage of sales methodology. Since a number of variables drive sales performance, reviewing the ratio of specific expenses to total sales could produce a more accurate indicator of sales performance. For example, compare sales by total advertising expenses or sales by sales person can provide useful information as sales performance drivers. Afterward, performing a correlation between expense categories would provide a reality check for budgeting. Below are a number of ways to review the effectiveness of specific sales events expense drivers from prior years:

- Sales by trade show efforts
- Sales by vendor telesales or inbound efforts
- Sales by trade publications and advertising
- Sales by direct response or direct mail
- Sales by web marketing
- Sales by account executive or manager
- Sales by specific demographic segments (if tracked and available)
- Sales by geographic segments (along with such a sales analysis, consider comparative year-over-year economic review of sales regions)

Trade show expenses		#Trade	Total		Name	Dates
Description	Expense	shows	expenses		New products trade show	Mar-13
Booth	4,500	4	$ 109,600		International trade show	Jun-13
Communications	1,500				Demo show	Sep-13
Collateral	2,500				Grand finale trade show	Nov-13
Registration	800					
Travel	400					
Lodging	5,000					
Meals	500					
Entertainment	1,200					
Staffing	5,000					
Temp help	2,500					
Advertising	3,500					
Insurance	1,000					
Catering	1,500					
Event planning	2,500					
Telecommunicatons	500					
Utilities	120					
Event decorator	1,000					
Seminar room reservations	500					
Event labor	250					

Figure 11.1 Sample trade show budget (see Microsoft Excel Business Budget Builder).

Figure 11.1 shows an example of how to identify specifically scheduled or anticipated events and project expenses for each one. The illustration in Figure 11.1 appears in the Sales and Marketing spreadsheet of the Microsoft Excel *Business Budget Builder* workbook.

Advertising Expenses

The key to successful brand recognition requires extensive promotion. Such promotion could include retaining professional service organizations such as an advertising agency or promotion firm. In addition, the various media and the internet have a variety of outlets for advertising and promotion, such as industry websites and banner and spot advertising promotions that make use of pay-per-click placement.

It is a good idea first to set specific objectives for product advertising and promotional events. Consider the sample objectives identified in Table 11.1, and develop those that fit your specific campaigns. Preparing a project plan that reflects an expense roll-up is a more accurate method

Table 11.1. Advertising and Promotion Campaign Objectives

Sales and marketing objectives	Time frame	Sales forecast	Costs
Increase company awareness and brand name recognition among enthusiast, retailers, buyers, and customer through an extensive advertising campaign in the xxxxxxx news media and internet banner placements four times monthly for the duration of the budgeted period			
Generate qualified sales leads and potential new distributors through telesales efforts			
Engage an advertising agency to create an extensive advertising program for supporting our new product line			
Attend three trade shows for making distributor contacts and direct response marketing agents			

Table 11.2. Objectives Worksheet

Objective:					
Task	Responsible	Start date	Completion date	Expense account	Expense amount

of determining outlays and expected sales revenues for the accomplishment of an objective. Table 11.2 shows an example of a simple project plan setup you can create in a spreadsheet for an objective. If the project requires staffing or capital equipment, ensure that you identify these in your staffing or capital plan.

Marketing and General and Administrative Expenses

As a safety check to determine if your expenses are sufficient for supporting sales efforts, consider historical expenses for the past 3 years.

Table 11.3. Historical Expense Analysis Budget Guidelines

1. Determine percentage of revenue or sales for each expense account from year to year.
2. Drill down into specific accounts within the above categories and review them individually.
3. What do monthly, quarterly, or annual trends tell you? Are there spikes?
4. Review the detail for marketing expenses to determine how much events (such as conferences, trade shows, conventions, and significant customer meetings) costs from year to year. Consider if you plan to engage in similar events for the budget year or if such events were single efforts.
5. Review the details for sales expenses for any trade publications used, employment of public relations firms, or radio, television, or newspaper advertising. Do you plan to have similar campaigns for the budget year or were they onetime efforts? Will you repeat these expenses at the same level?
6. Review general and administrative expense accounts and consider the following questions: a. Did they support customer efforts? b. Were they onetime expenses that will not repeat? c. Which are equal streams of payments like rent, leases, automobile payments, or insurance? d. Do these payments increase from year to year? e. Do any of them need evaluation for renewal or a new bid?
7. Are any expenses for outsourced products or services part of KMAs™ or the organization chart?

Historical expenses may or may not be a good indicator for forecasting. However, such use depends on the approach you took in prior years or if you engaged in budgeting in the past. If you have not prepared a budget for prior years, your company's expenses could swing widely for certain expense accounts such as travel, trade shows, conventions, and collateral. A financial statement's historical review for expenses can be revealing for identifying trends and expenses that may not have contributed to customer attainment and retention efforts. Consequently, when conducting such a review for baseline purposes, use the guidelines in Table 11.3.

These expense analyses serve as parameters for prior years' performance decisions. They supply several useful purposes for an upcoming budget:

- They identify general and administrative expenses for managing the business.
- They reveal areas for improved expense management.

- They identify expenses related to contracts or agreements that may or may not be needed in the future.
- They show where objectives may need to be established.
- They reveal required versus discretionary or optional spending patterns.
- They identify expenses related to specific projects.

Communications

Communications can be a significant expense due to the use of all the high technology tools necessary to keep in touch with customers, vendors, and other constituents. Communications (or telecommunications) expenses consist of those shown in Table 11.4. Depending on your organizational structure and responsibility oversight, a large portion of these expenses may belong to one organizational budget, such as IT or Finance with a budget team manager (CIO) representing the organization. The IT organization has the expertise to determine company requirements for internal and external network equipments, services, and subscriptions.

Having it report to the office of the CFO is even more natural if it is an outsourced component. Its organizational arrangement can have a significant bearing on expense considering the capital equipment outlay necessary for supporting telecommunications infrastructure. Furthermore,

Table 11.4. Communications Expenses

Communication expenses to consider
Telephone (both landline, cells phone services) and teleconference connectivity services
Internet and email
Fax services
Internal and Intranet company networks
Virtual Private Network (VPN)
FTP upload systems
WebEx or other conferencing cloud applications
After-hours answering services
Internal communications device subscription services
Enterprise marketing and customer relationship management subscriptions

contractual arrangement for outsourced company components is a financial matter for control and safeguards purposes. In your review, be aware of the outsourced criteria listed in Table C.1 of Appendix C.

Leases and Expenses

The two most common types of leases to consider for budgeting consist of: (1) fair market value or operating lease and (2) finance or capital lease. Transactions for operating leases are expensed and should be budgeted accordingly for all your equipment under operating leases. Capital leases fall under capital equipment with Finance having responsibility for its classification, management, depreciation, and reporting. For capital leases, there is a purchase option at the end of the lease. Capital leases are classified as fixed assets on the balance sheet. Budgeted payments for capital lease loans are under two accounts: liability accounts (Notes Payable or Loans) on the balance sheet for the principal portion and the interest expense account for the interest portion.

If you use the Microsoft Excel *Business Budget Builder* workbook, enter all operating leases payments in the Parameters Setup spreadsheet as shown in Table 11.5.

Enter capital lease equipment in the Capital Budget spreadsheet as shown in Table 11.6 and the corresponding loan amounts in the

Table 11.5. Microsoft Excel Workbook Equipment Lease Monthly Payments Entry

Equipment lease monthly payments	
High speed printer	$ 650
High speed copier	$ 700
Assembly Router	$ 700
TOTAL EQUIP LEASING	$ 2,050

Table 11.6. Microsoft Excel Business Budget Builder Workbook Capital Budget Asset Entry

Asset Class	Description	Purchase Price	Cost Basis	Current Placed in Service Date	Recovery Period in Years	Section 179/ Bonus	Accumulated Depreciation	Balance	Annual Depreciation	Monthly Depreciation
Machinery & Equipment	Current	250,000	235,000	Dec-13	7	15,000	45,500	189,500	29,377	2,448
Furniture, Fixtures, Cellular Phones	Current	100,000	80,000	Dec-13	7	20,000	13,500	66,500	10,309	859
Autos and Other Listed Property	Current	56,000	46,000	Dec-13	7	10,000	10,650	35,350	1,875	156
Autos and Other Listed Property	Ford Ranger	25,500	15,000	Jan-14	7	10,500		15,000	3,150	263
Autos and Other Listed Property	Ford Van	45,000	34,500	May-14	7	10,500		34,500	3,150	263
Autos and Other Listed Property			-					-	-	-
Autos and Other Listed Property			-					-	-	-
Autos and Other Listed Property			-					-	-	-
Autos and Other Listed Property			-					-	-	-
Autos and Other Listed Property										
Buildings	Current	500,000	500,000	Dec-13	27.5		125,000	375,000	14,798	1,233
Land	Current	125,000	125,000	Dec-13	0			125,000	-	-
Leasehold Improvement	Current	55,000	55,000	Dec-13	15		13,500	41,500	3,002	250
Organizational & Startup Costs	Current	12,500	12,500	Dec-13	15		10,000	2,500	181	15
Goodwill	Current	45,000	45,000	Dec-13	15		32,500	12,500	904	75
Computers	Current	15,000	15,000	Dec-13	5		7,500	7,500	1,628	136
Software	Current	3,500	3,500	Dec-13	3		2,300	1,200	434	36
Computers	Current	15,000	13,000	Dec-13	5	2,000	-	13,000	2,821	235

Table 11.7. Micro Excel Business Budget Builder Workbook Notes Payable Entry

Notes payable balances	Current	Long term
Longshore Bank	205,000	1,400,000
ABC Commercial Bank	75,000	325,000
State Bank lease loan	125,000	
Totals	$ 405,000	$ 1,725,000

Parameters Setup spreadsheet in the table called Notes Payable Balances as shown in Table 11.7.

For tracking the lease loan interest for a capital lease, it is preferable to set up the interest expense account for capital equipment leases as a sub-account under interest expenses. In this way, you can budget the remaining portion of the capital lease for the budgeted period and track actual transactions against it during the fiscal period.

Automobile Expenses

Automobiles you own and place in service or those you lease will drive their expenses. These expenses include gas, maintenance, repairs, registration, and related expenses. For tax reporting purposes, you may wish to budget insurance premium expenses for automobiles under insurance expenses. Keep in mind that expenses associated with company vehicles occur simultaneous to placement of the asset in service. For example, if you budget the purchase of a new vehicle for your business in June 2013, any expenses related to its use or maintenance should also be budgeted beginning in the same month. Finance is normally responsible for allocating any depreciation expenses for these capital assets. If you financed automobiles, make sure you enter any loan amounts in the Notes Payable Balances table on the Budget Parameters Setup spreadsheet (see Table 11.7). For budgeting purposes, automobiles receive similar treatment as any other equipment leases. However, terms and conditions may differ.

Travel

Travel could be a major expense, especially for sales, marketing, or customer-support requirements. Travel, meals, and entertainment have several different expense activities:

1. Expenses directly related to marketing and sales efforts. These include trips to schedule marketing events such as trade shows, conventions, and related events
2. Sales call expenses
3. Travel to customer sites for installation of products, warranty calls, onsite customer work, and related activities
4. Travel to conduct business
5. Meals and entertainment for employee benefits

It is easier to have a single budget for all travel and not be concerned about budgeting meals and entertainment separately unless these comprise a large expense, such as for large company events. When budgeting for travel expenses, it is a good idea to align these expenses with any undertaken business events to which these expenses relate, such as trade shows, conventions, customer visits, and employee events. After completing budget allocation in their respective budgeted periods, conduct a review to ensure that these expenses align with the appropriate events.

Facilities Requirements and Management

Facilities management ranks high on the list of management. Whether you are a professional services business or in manufacturing or retail, the facilities management budget is critical to business operations. The following checklist will provide you with items to consider for your facilities budget.

1. Lease agreements (whether you lease the facilities to others or lease it yourself)
2. Repairs and maintenance
3. Leasehold or tenant improvements (a capitalized asset)
4. Facilities services (utilities, janitorial, and maintenance)
5. Equipment maintenance
6. Security and monitoring
7. Liability coverage
8. Regulatory compliance
9. Property taxes

Insurance Coverage Expense

Risk is one of the major drivers for budgeting insurance, and insurance budgeting requirements depends on type of business, industry, and risks to your business. Once you finalize your budgeted sales, you may wish to discuss your liability and worker's compensation insurance requirements with your broker to determine sufficiency of coverage. Insurance coverage also includes expenses for the following:

- Health and vision
- Life- and long-term disability for you and your employees
- Key personnel insurance
- Business interruption or continuity insurance

Accounting and Legal

Accounting and legal expenses will depend on whether you manage them internally or if they are outsourced components. A review of Appendix C in terms of contractual arrangement and the cost benefit of maintaining them internally is an important first step. Depending on the size of your company, outsourcing the accounting component comes with risks. Some of these risks include the following:

1. Timeliness in reporting for decision-making and corrective action (Does outsourced expenses far outweigh staffing internally?)

2. The outsourced entities involvement with and knowledge of operations and the business model
3. The disconnection of budgeting from the outsourced entity and tracking actual expenses to budget
4. The exposure of financial information and corresponding strategy
5. The challenge in making regular adjustments as required to inventories and other balance sheet accounts
6. The risks in segregation of duties with the outsourced accounting or bookkeeping entity

Read the entire Appendix C for considering safeguards for vendor relationships and their corresponding contractual costs.

CHAPTER 12

Total Staffing Plan

When machines replace all humans, who will manage the machines?

Identifying Staffing Criteria

Prior to reading this chapter, perform a quick review of Chapter 7, "Key Management Areas: Budgeting Foundations." The staffing plan is a large segment of the budget team manager's total budget plan. The drivers for the staffing plan are

1. the organization's support for marketing and sales;
2. the objectives the budget team member sets for the organization;
3. resource requirements for both direct and indirect labor to meet product and service delivery capacity demand;
4. whether you outsource some organizational components; and
5. the management of outsourced components.

Once each budget team manager completes the staffing plan based on full time equivalent (FTE), part time labor, and temporary staffing plan, the staffing plan considers the costs of staffing and if outsourcing will be more cost effective and more productive option. The staffing plan examines current staffing and requirements to support the sales and marketing plan or in support of producing products and services. This examination means an analysis of the existing organizational structure for determining sufficiency of human resources to support objectives and the work linked to them.

The staffing plan considers burden costs associated with staffing such as taxes, benefits, insurance, and related expenses. Finally, the staffing plan includes a hiring plan for determining when payroll and related costs will occur based on sales forecasts.

Best Practices for Organizational Staffing

Consider the following variables in developing your total staffing plan:

1. Full time equivalent, part time, and temporary staffing requirements
2. Base compensation
3. Job descriptions
4. Objectives and performance measurements
5. Cross training and work coverage

Figure 12.1 gives an example for a complete staffing plan from the Staffing Plan spreadsheet in the *Business Budget Builder* Microsoft Excel workbook. Best practices for determining staffing requirements begin with the work performed, job descriptions, and stated objectives.

Thomas Bechet compares the tradition staff planning to a strategic one and concludes that the traditional methodology falls short in many areas. He emphasizes that strategic staffing accounts for the "implication of change" that considers staffing levels, capabilities, current availability, prospective supply, anticipated versus forecasted supply, and the need to close talent gap and deal with surpluses.[1] He suggests that the traditional approach to staffing is inadequate because it uses a job-specific template approach that includes a 3-year roll-up for a total headcount. He contends that this method often misses the mark and is not realistic, involving much more work than necessary. His staffing solution considers several components. The more important ones from a budgeting perspective consist of the following:[2]

- Have a proactive planning perspective
- Focus on issues
- Consider the process
- Keep plans separate rather than consolidating (I would suggest a separate as well as a consolidation approach for pro forma purposes)
- Conduct scenario and "what if" planning

While these points are noteworthy for implementation in a budget plan, they also should include structuring, purpose, and description. The next section discusses these three approaches.

Figure 12.1. Staffing plan example (see Microsoft Excel Business Budget Builder).

Staffing, Compensation, and Job Descriptions

One primary task that best identifies human resources for work performed is the development of job descriptions. A major task associated with this event is to review the job descriptions related with those roles for determining if they encompass the responsibilities you identified in your resources charter. The key to writing well-defined job descriptions is following the steps below:

1. Defining the mission of your organization—The company as a whole and its subsidiary components have missions. Your organization's mission should be in alignment with the company as a whole.
2. Identify the KMAs in your organization and write a description of each. How does each one of the KMA contribute to the company's mission and objectives? Review Chapter 7 concerning the development of KMAs for budgeting budget resources. It is at this level where you define resource requirements.
3. What staffing do you need for each KMA?
4. Write a job description for each position within your organization.

Once you have prepared this review, this makes it easier to identify resource requirements and their corresponding funding for the budget. Will you be needing part time or temporary staffing at specific times when it is not cost effective to hire someone full time? This review accomplishes three goals:

1. Clarifies role responsibilities in support of customer efforts
2. Helps to identify gaps that may need to be filled for supporting customer efforts
3. Helps to determine resources for KMA management

Job descriptions are the fundamental building blocks for the ability to allocate funding to business resources. They are not just documents that sit on shelves or guide team managers in their jobs. Two of their primary purposes are to explain the reason for a position's role in the business and to determine how that role supports business mission and objective.

Linking staffing back to business mission and objectives makes the staffing plan strategic as a resource outcome. Job descriptions clarify staffing roles and responsibilities in the company's strategy.

If you do not have written job descriptions, the early stages of the budget cycle is a good time to develop them. If job descriptions currently exist in some form, review and modify them to accommodate the guidelines for the tasks and responsibilities associated with the KMAs. The job description should act as a process guide for work performance. Keep sensitive information separate, such as pay scale and related issues. For more information on writing effective job descriptions, consult www.amazon.com or the local bookstore for books on developing them. Margie Mader-Clark authored an excellent book, *The Job Description Handbook*, accompanied with a CD available from Amazon (http://amzn. to/LI2Lj6) for writing job descriptions.

When preparing your staffing plan, keep in mind the increased number of individuals who remain with a company for a long period is more the exception than the rule. In addition, consider accommodation for any long-term absence due to sickness or other reasons in your plan. This is not only true for individual staff but also true for managerial and executive staff. Tim Frame recommends including overlap or cross training in the plan.[3] This also ensures that you are not left in a knowledge base deficiency or short of resources when such events occur.

CHAPTER 13

Pro Forma Financial Statements

The financial statements are a goal-setting paradise. Set these goals early for preventing your statements from being a nightmare.

Objectives

Upon completing this chapter, you will be able to prepare a complete set of pro forma financial statements. More often than not, your accounting system will have this capability after you enter all the necessary account data.

Pro Forma Financial Statements

The outcome of the budget process is the development of the pro forma financial statements. This chapter applies the rule of 10 for laying out the goals of the pro forma financial statements for the purpose of budgeting or forecasting:

1. To cast a vision and give financial direction for a business
2. To provide a roadmap for company success
3. To offer leadership (especially the board of directors and executives) with a quantifiable and measurable plan for business initiatives, ventures, and opportunities
4. To set specific objectives related to revenues, expenses, funding requirements, and the management of assets, liabilities, invested capital, and cash flow
5. To give shareholders assurance in the company's ability to execute initiatives proactively, address risks, and provide clarity for business direction

6. To give confidence to lending or investing entities in the knowledge and ability of the company to execute the plan successfully

7. To quantify and measure the business plan and strategy based on certain assumptions about the market, economy, and internal operations

8. To enable executives and managers to set performance standards for responsibility and accountability

9. To aid management in making informed current decisions about anticipated events and business transactions

10. To give financial guidance for all staff

The purpose of this chapter is to give general guidance and consideration for their development. Since you have already engaged in detailed analysis and preparation of specific categories related to the income statement, this chapter suggests particular areas of concern related to the information they present and their use. This book assumes the reader is sufficiently familiar with the financial statements so that a detailed analysis of the pro forma statements is unnecessary.

From an executive position, an annual snapshot (or vertical analysis) of all three statements provides performance measurements for the budgeted period. It considers the ratio of cost of sales and operating expenses to revenue on the income statement and the ratio of specific values on the balance sheet or income statement to other values on the same statements. See Chapter 14, for some of the more widely used financial ratios and a discussion on their use for measuring financial performance.

Using industry financial ratios with pro forma financial statements allows you to conduct a "sanity check" on how your company compares with your competitors in your industry. Such an analytical check gives useful information for determining where you need improvements in your financial condition for becoming more competitive. For example, if your Acid Test (quick) ratio for your prepared pro forma balance sheet (available cash within 30 days of liquidity divided by current liabilities) is substantially lower than the industry average, you are projecting a weakness in the ability to compete. If your budgeted balance sheet projects a lower ratio, it reflects a deterioration of near-term liquid assets to meet obligations. This projects competitive weakness in the ability to finance sales efforts.

This portrayal is an indicator to revisit your pro forma analysis for determining the basis of your projections. If the basis of your projections indeed reflects such weaknesses, then re-examine your strategy and supporting objectives. If your basis is derived from historical trends, this could be an indicator of relying too much on a baseline (historical financial performance) and the need for improvement initiatives for inclusion in your budget. Such an analysis should be undertaken first. It can shed light on your current financial position compared to where you want to be.

From a management activity perspective, trends are important for tracking and measuring performance. This calls for a horizontal analysis as shown in Figure 13.1. You might want to ensure that your pro forma financial statements include monthly and perhaps quarterly projections. Quarterly projections are especially important if you are a publicly traded company and must file the 10-Q with the SEC.

This horizontal analysis allows you to examine trends that reflect significant differences in actual revenue and expenditures when compared to budget. After you implement the budget and conduct comparisons to actual financial data, variances enable you to identify any financial issues or challenges. From this variance analysis, you can delve into root causes and make the appropriate corrective actions and any necessary re-forecasts. Are there spikes in revenues or spending in a particular period? The budgeted income statement leads to their discovery.

After you complete the pro forma income statement, your next step is the pro forma balance sheet. Your goal is to derive ending balances for all balance sheet accounts. The best place to begin are the cash accounts. Tying respective balance sheet accounts to specific objectives allows you to be proactive in their management.

For example, you determine that slow-paying customers has a negative influence on financing specific critical projects that led your company to obtain additional line of credit. You establish an objective for days sales outstanding (DSO) of 35 days and set up incentives for customers to pay faster by offering 2.5% Net 30 terms. You also determine that offering these terms would cost you less than financing the additional line of credit and that it would increase cash flow.

Setting such targets with other balance sheet accounts enables you to improve their management and management of your balance sheet

Operating Budget

MONTH	Jan-14	Feb-14	Mar-14	Apr-14	May-14	Jun-14	Jul-14	Aug-14	Sep-14	Oct-14	Nov-14	Dec-14	TOTALS	% SALES
INCOME STATEMENT														
TOTAL OPERATING REVENUE	$ 823,192	$ 856,489	$ 889,786	$ 923,083	$ 956,380	$ 989,677	$ 1,022,974	$ 1,055,821	$ 1,089,418	$ 1,122,715	$ 1,156,162	$ 819,874	11,705,565	
NET REVENUES	$ 823,192	$ 856,489	$ 889,786	$ 923,083	$ 956,380	$ 989,677	$ 1,022,974	$ 1,055,821	$ 1,089,418	$ 1,122,715	$ 1,156,162	$ 819,874	$ 11,705,565	
TOTAL COST OF GOODS SOLD	$ 474,831	$ 481,856	$ 507,063	$ 528,213	$ 563,072	$ 598,077	$ 605,967	$ 627,582	$ 645,540	$ 663,304	$ 681,110	$ 506,517	$ 6,873,132	59%
GROSS PROFIT	$ 348,361	$ 374,633	$ 382,723	$ 394,870	$ 393,307	$ 401,600	$ 417,006	$ 428,239	$ 443,878	$ 459,410	$ 475,051	$ 313,357	$ 4,832,433	41%
OPERATING EXPENSES														
TOTAL RESEARCH & DEVELOPMENT	141,509	134,100	69,100	69,100	69,100	69,100	74,100	79,100	73,089	73,089	73,089	76,518	1,000,996	9%
TOTAL SALES & MARKETING	$ 144,001	$ 139,002	$ 149,003	$ 132,004	$ 133,505	$ 139,006	$ 136,507	$ 151,008	$ 139,009	$ 134,510	$ 128,211	$ 101,412	$ 1,627,178	14%
TOTAL GENERAL & ADMINISTRATIVE	71,145	86,145	81,314	85,444	93,730	100,394	99,526	105,133	106,151	106,641	106,641	111,426	1,153,689	10%
TOTAL OPERATING EXPENSES	831,486	841,102	806,479	814,761	859,408	896,577	916,101	962,823	963,789	977,546	989,052	795,872	10,654,995	91%
OPERATING INCOME	(8,294)	15,386	83,306	108,321	96,972	93,099	106,872	92,998	125,629	145,170	167,110	24,001	1,050,570	9%
NET OTHER INCOME	(16,240)	(25,457)	(52,059)	(61,800)	(57,250)	(55,638)	(60,961)	(55,418)	(88,152)	(75,742)	(84,274)	(27,942)	(640,934)	-5%
NET EARNINGS	(24,535)	(10,071)	31,247	46,521	39,722	37,461	45,912	37,580	57,477	69,428	82,836	(3,941)	409,636	3%
NET EARNINGS %	-3%	-1%	4%	5%	4%	4%	4%	4%	5%	6%	7%	0%	3%	

Figure 13.1. Horizontal trend statement of earnings analysis.

and cash flow to budget. Loan amortization schedules offer sound budget management tools by providing you with information for budgeting interest expenses and beginning and ending balances for your budgeted balance sheet. The same holds true with your company being the lender. Providing amortization schedules to the borrower allows you to set budget amounts for these asset balances and interest income. As a process management tool, they also enable you to exercise substantial management control over cash and risk reduction.

Other Income Statement Budget Considerations

As you develop the pro forma financial statements, a number of considerations, sometimes omitted, could lead to significant variances during the budget year. This section provides a checklist of those items so that they are not overlooked.

1. Capital Gains and Losses—This line item arises when you dispose of capital equipment or discontinued operations. If you anticipate any disposition by sale or otherwise disposal of equipment upon budgeting for new equipment, ensure that you include its gain or loss in the budget.

    Discontinued operations would normally be anticipated so that you would know to include it in your budget. See Financial Accounting Standard (FAS) 144 for treatment and reporting of discontinued operations. The disclosure of such anticipation rests on the timeframe for its disposition. You need to consider the following two transactions in your budget for discontinued operations:

    a. The income or loss from such discontinued operations
    b. The loss or gain in the sale of the discontinued operation

2. Interest Expenses—Ensure that you take into account all short- and long-term debt in preparing your budget. Cost of money can be a sizable amount on outstanding debt, credit cards, or outstanding lines of credit.

3. Interest or Other Income—This category is easy to omit since it may not be material. However, establishing a budget for other income

encompasses more than interest or dividends on savings, securities, or other investments. For example, nonoperating income such as the sale of noninventory assets above basis cost, rent income, or foreign exchange could lead to a substantial variance if they are not budgeted. Review prior year data for a history that would lead you to anticipate activity for such income.

4. Canceled Debts—Do you anticipate any cancellation of debt for the budget period? If so, ensure that you budget it.

5. Royalties—Unless you are a business that pays or receives royalties, you will not need to be concerned about this expense or income. If you are a publisher, then it will be a substantial budget item.

Budgets Setting on a Shelf Gather Dust

Allergies to dust are preferable to allergy to budgets; at least with the latter, you have a plan before you realize what's coming.

CHAPTER 14

Execution Plan

Execute your budget, not your people.

The execution plan is the most often missed segment of the budget. To be able to stay on target with business objectives, you must have an execution plan. The execution plan is essentially a project that the Project Leader (or CFO) continues to lead after the completion of the budget. The execution plan lays out the implementation of the budget. This implementation has several critical elements:

1. The progress of objectives and corresponding actions and milestones, revenue, and costs associated with them
2. Status of issues and challenges for meeting objectives
3. Status meeting preparation and their agenda
4. Financial performance status
5. Corrective actions or re-forecasts

Prerequisites to Budget Status Meetings

Having regular status meetings insure that your company stays on target for meeting the objectives the team sets. Having a regular schedule for month end close with cut-off times for accounting activity allows you to move straight into financial status review routinely. It also allows for timely reporting to financial institutions and to the SEC for publicly held companies. Under the Sarbanes-Oxley Act of 2002, the CEO and CFO of publicly traded companies must certify the financial statements and accompanying disclosures.

Meeting reporting deadlines places a high priority on ensuring that publicly held companies hold to an appropriate month-end close deadline schedule and make it consistent from period to period. Of course, quarterly and annual reporting requires much more preparation because of the reporting requirements for publicly held companies. That is the reason why transaction activity cut-off is highly critical for timely financial reporting. If you plan to go public, setting up an efficient and timely month-end close schedule well ahead of any IPO makes for a smooth transition toward becoming a publicly held company. The importance of doing so is twofold:

1. It establishes sound internal controls for becoming a publicly held company, among which are
   a. sound budgeting and reporting mechanisms;
   b. establishing and reporting on key metrics;
   c. focal point for investor relations; and
   d. preparation for a greater degree of financial disclosures.
2. As a rule, going public requires audited financial statements for the 3 years prior to filing an IPO.

Setting up month-end close and financial reporting routines places your business in the position to accomplish these two goals as well as timely reporting to meet legal reporting deadlines. It also enables you to conduct timely regular discussions and review around budgets compared to actual financial data so you can take corrective actions when needed and stay on top of business performance.

If you do not have a regular month-end close calendar with all tasks identified and all responsible parties contributing to a deadline, this book recommends setting one up even if you do not anticipate filing an IPO. To ensure that your month-end close does not omit any critical activity, set up a task list with each activity associated to a date deadline. Remember that several tasks have dependencies, so it is important to reflect activity that depends on others completing their work. If you are a small company, most month-end closing activities reside in Finance. In the manufacturing or retail environment, several activities have critical cut-offs, such as closing work orders, conducting cycle counts, reclassifying inventories, allocating indirect overhead, and booking accruals. All of these and related activities must be completed prior to the preparation of the financial statements for review against the period budgets and the preparation of the financial statements and reporting package.

Budget Meetings and the Budget Execution Plan

The budget execution plan has a well-defined monthly, quarterly, and annual financial review cycle. It is the critical ongoing activity after the final budget. The execution plan is the means for the budget team to communicate with one another on important financial management issues and status relative to company objectives and mission. In addition to the completed financial statements and associated disclosures (whether for publicly held, private equity, or privately owned concerns), the budget execution plan also includes discussion around measurements for financial performance. This book concentrates only on three types of measurements:

1. Established budgets
2. Benchmarks
3. Objectives

This chapter discusses established budgets and benchmarks. Chapter 5 provides a discussion on setting objectives as targets for performance.

While having at least monthly meetings on financial performance is important, team interaction and communication daily on performance issues provide for a much quicker response to issues and challenges that may arise. Waiting until month end frequently does not afford a timely response to critical issues currently in process. Budget team members and the executive team need a readily available knowledge base for tracking present performance and for responding to customer and competitive issues. Informal daily meetings on business critical issues, action items, and follow up keeps everyone informed on progress, performance, and needed decisions.

Brown suggests that available financial data should include three forms of data: (1) historical, (2) current, and (3) future.[1] While he refers to historical data as "water under the bridge," he highlights the critical need for present data for responding to financial conditions with informed decisions, such as pipeline orders, current receivables, and daily sales numbers.[2]

Brown again recommends that success depends on

- the capacity to access the "true costs of processes and products/ services";
- financial metrics that cover past, present, and future;
- financial statistics "tightly linked to key success factors"; and
- continuous evaluation of financial metrics to fit your company's ability to measure relevant data for successful decisions.[3]

In other words, the financial database needs the capability to provide a wide range of data in useful formats for informed decisions at all levels of the organization. These data includes not only financial but also nonfinancial data and metrics. If such a database in your company does not have this capability, the budget process is the place for performing upgrades to meet data and metric measurement requirements for sound management decisions.

Established Budgets

In certain respects, budgets are the internal set of benchmarks against which you measure financial performance. They arise out of your external and internal strategic assumptions and the specific objectives you set for the budgeted period. While budgets provide very strong targets for focusing your company and measuring results, they need parameter guidelines. Benchmarks and objectives provide those parameters as much as shoulders and the middle line of a street or freeway establish borders and markings for driving your automobile (see the illustration in Figure 14.1). Objectives point out the direction, while benchmarks establish the borders.

Benchmarks

When establishing your budgets, one way of providing a reality check and for setting financial performance goals is to use key industry financial ratios as measurements for your pro forma budgeted financial statements. This ensures that when you develop and review your budgets, you have

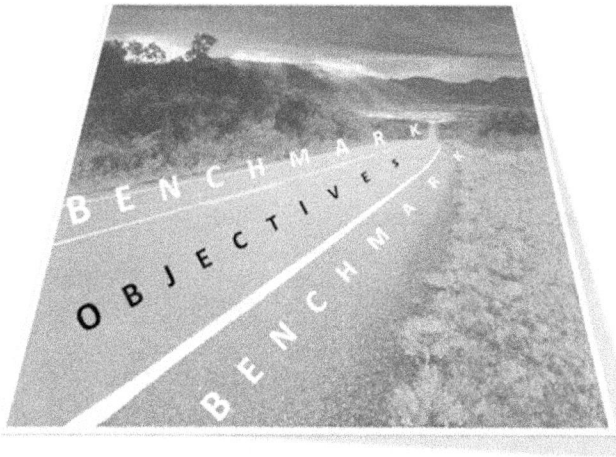

Figure 14.1. Benchmarks and objectives as budget parameters.

a reliable alignment for the financial statements: your industry and the revenue size of other companies in your industry.

For example, after the first draft of the budget and preparation of the pro forma financial statements, the CFO can compare the ratios for the pro forma financial statements to industry ratio benchmarks. If your statement ratios are lower than industry benchmarks, you may wish to consider if the budget reflects competitive reality. If rework is not feasible due to your current financial condition falling below industry benchmarks, the industry benchmark ratios will provide you with targets for strengthening your financial condition over a given set of periods. You would then know the areas and kind of objectives to set for reaching specific targets. This methodology is simply one of many ways you can benefit from industry financial ratios.

Such use of industry benchmarks give you benefit by not only revealing business performance strengths and weaknesses but also showing how you stack up against your competitors. You can also use this information in developing a strong competitive analysis during the course of preparing sales and marketing budgets. That is, the industry benchmark data reflects the financial performance of your competition for your size business. If industry financial ratios show you to be in a position of weakness compared to competitors, this information could inform your business strategy and corresponding budgets.

In his article, "Achieving High Performance: the Value of Benchmarking," Chuck Wise from Accenture Management Consulting identifies four "critical benefits for organizations looking to improve performance":[4]

1. Current state assessment
2. Foundation for transformation programs
3. Strong basis for continuous improvement
4. A set of terms and definitions for company processes

He also notes that benchmarking is also a gap identifier between a company's current state and end goal.[5] Benchmarks as roadmaps to high achievement are foundational to his overall message.

Several companies provide subscription services for obtaining industry financial statements ratio benchmarks. One leader in the industry for such a subscription service is *The Risk Management Association* (RMA).[6] Table 14.1 identifies several highly useful ratios for benchmarking your pro forma budgeted financial statements and prepared financial statements for period performance. For a description of other ratios important to business decision-making, consult *The McGraw-Hill Pocket Guide to Business Finance*.[7] This book covers 201 financial measurements used widely by financial institutions, analysts, investors, and business executives for making decisions on financing, growth, investments, problem solving, and interpretation of financial statements results.

Such a book combined with a subscription for financial statements benchmarking services will equip you to measure business performance and grow your business according to your stated targets. Since all industries are different, there is no one-size-fits-all set of ratios for measuring business performance as reflected in the financial statements. That is the reason why obtaining a subscription is the most reasonable means of attaining a reality check on your business performance.

You can also develop internal benchmarking by performing an analysis of prior years. Internal benchmarking could offer a more realistic measurement for financial performance. You can apply the ratios in Table 14.1 to actual internal financial statements data over several consecutive periods (such as 4–6 years) for deriving benchmarks from them. Your company may not have a direct comparison with others in your

Table 14.1. Financial Performance Ratios

Financial ratio	Description
Current Ratio Current assets/current liabilities	This measures the ability to meet current liability obligations from current assets.
Quick Ratio (Acid test) Cash and other short term liquid accounts (money market, A/R/current liabilities)	The acid test applies a more stringent measurement of liquidity for meeting current obligations. This should not fall below 1:1 ratio, but industry is a better determinant.
Cash Ratios Cash ratio = Cash + marketable securities (money market)/current obligations—Immediate convertibility of cash for meeting current obligations. Cash flow-dividends/capital equipment expenditures—This identifies cash sufficiency to maintain fixed assets from cash rather than from borrowings. Cash flow/Total debt—This ratio identifies cash to satisfy total debt obligations. This is an indicator of solvency.	A number of cash ratios that you could apply to financial performance analysis. This table reviews three essential ones: 1. Cash ratio; 2. Cash-to-capital-equipment expenditure ratio; 3. Cash flow to total bdebt.
Sales (net)/Trade receivables	Measures trade receivables turnover with a higher ratio indicating a shorter convertibility time of receivables to cash
DSO 365 (366)/Sales/Trade receivables	Informs concerning the number of days trade receivables are outstanding and collection efficiency.
Inventory Turnover 365 (366)/Cost of sales/Average inventory (where average inventory = Beginning inventory + Ending inventory)/2	Provides an indicator of how quickly inventory converts to sales. A lower than benchmark ratio indicates slow sales and the risk of excess and obsolete inventory. A higher than benchmark ratio could reveal a risk of shortage and delivery to customers. Inventory management strikes a balance through using a sound MRP system.

(*Continued*)

Table 14.1. Financial Performance Ratios (Continued)

Financial ratio	Description
Inventory Turnover = Cost of sales/average inventory (where average inventory = Beginning inventory-ending inventory/2)	A low ratio could be an indicator of slow sales or inventory excess and obsolescence (E&O).
Profit Margin Sales—expenses	Measures profit performance. A trend of several quarters is a better indicator than one or two months due to seasonality or spikes in sales or expenses. Combine this ratio with your budget to benchmark how well you perform compared to your goals as well as compared to those in your industry.
Return on Assets Net Sales/Average Total Assets (where Average total assets = Beginning total assets − Ending total assets)	Return on assets reflects the company's ability to generate profit from assets.
Return on Equity (ROE) Net income/Average stockholder equity	There are a number of equity ratios as indicators of how the company performs with invested capital. ROE is a telling sign of a company's strength as well as attractiveness to investors. Combine this ratio with how well you perform compared to budget benchmarks for gauging your company's success in meeting targets. ROE should play a role in your assumption and objectives.

industry, so the use of internal benchmarks could be a more reliable indicator for both your budgets and historical financial performance analysis. Using internal and industry benchmarks will aid the CFO in giving you more information in discussions over decisions and necessary corrective actions in your financial status meetings during the budget period.

Be alert to one weakness in relying on internal benchmarks. A weak historical financial condition may lead you to establish benchmarks that reflect any financial weaknesses. However, comparing internal benchmarks to industry ones and setting ratio targets can overcome this weakness.

Take care to examine historical financial statements for large swings in revenue and expenses and their causes. In addition, when reviewing the balance sheet, consider the drivers for the various line items, such as trade payables and receivables, fixed assets, short- or long-term notes, other assets, and liabilities. They could skew financial indicators and be misleading as benchmarks. By eliminating or ignoring large swings in historical data, you can smooth out historical trends and derive a more realistic set of data for developing internal financial ratio benchmarks. Treating large swings in this manner assumes that they are nonrecurring.

Furthermore, comparing the internal benchmarks with industry benchmarks provide you a more balanced approach for financial benchmarking. For example, if industry financial ratios were higher than your internal benchmarks for the current ratio, this would lead you to determine cash flow drivers for adjusting budget numbers or setting eventual targets.

Once you complete your budget in the *Business Budget Builder* Microsoft Excel workbook, this budgeting application automatically provides you with a set of financial ratios in seven categories. See Figure 14.2, for examples of financial ratios appearing in the Financial Ratios spreadsheet. This spreadsheet is set up for entering industry ratios for comparing to those generated from your financial statements. Simply enter them in the column to the right of the generated ratios as shown in Figure 14.2. The book previously cited, *The McGraw-Hill Pocket Guide to Business Finance*, offers an interpretation of the ratios appearing in the Financial Ratios spreadsheet located in the *Business Budget Builder* Microsoft Excel workbook. The RMA offers interpretive publications on its website (see endnote[6]).

Liquidity ratios		
	Company	Industry
Current ratio	2.87	
Quick ratio	2.80	
Cash ratio	1.72	
A/R turnover	6.72	
Days in receivables	54.35	
Net sales to net working capital	4.09	
Cost of sales to inventory	7.90	
Inventory turnover	44.34	
Days in inventory	8.23	
Cost of sales to accounts payable	0.92	
Days in accounts payable	58.65	

Profitability indicator ratios		
	Company	Industry
Profit margin analysis	19%	
Effective tax rate	39%	
Return on assets	22%	
Return on equity	37%	
Return on capital employed	54%	

Operating performance ratios		
	Company	Industry
Sales per employee	$ 409,807	
Total asset turnover (times)	1.25	
Return on net worth	41.61%	
Return on total assets	24%	

Figure 14.2. Financial statements ratios generator (see Microsoft Excel Business Budget Builder).

CHAPTER 15

Period Ending Financial Reviews

Review what you have executed, and execute after you review.

Financial and Business Performance Reviews

Period ending financial reviews are major segments of the budget execution plan. During the course of the budget period, financial reviews occur on a regular basis. They are a necessary part of the budget cycle in that the prepared budget guides the actual performance. Consequently, historical financial reviews have an important managerial role for ensuring that actual performance aligns with stated objectives as measured by the pro forma financial statements. Regardless of company size, legal structure, or industry, regular financial reviews are an imperative for the following reasons:

1. Providing a regular disciplined managerial mechanism for measuring financial performance
2. Informing shareholders and executive management of financial performance and condition
3. Insuring financial performance aligns with business strategy[1]
4. Identifying business decisions for ensuring that they are in line with company objectives (this item is different from point 3 in that it focuses on examining decisions)
5. Providing a mechanism for preventing financial surprises
6. Reviewing financial soundness
7. Determining cash flow adequacy for use of funds and meeting financial obligations

Monthly intervals are the most preferred. Any longer intervals may not afford a company the opportunity to respond to financial performance issues in sufficient time to make the necessary business decisions or take corrective actions. Waiting especially until the conclusion of the budget year for preparing your taxes defeats the purpose of budgeting. It also does not afford the business sufficient time for making immediate financial decisions when needed to encounter changing market conditions or any deteriorating financial conditions. Financial reviews do not discount daily and weekly financial status updates and tactical discussions concerning performance. Such regular updates naturally lead into informed monthly, quarterly, and annual financial and business performance reviews.

This is especially true with smaller businesses or startup enterprises. They are in a vulnerable position because of limited resources to meet market opportunity. Furthermore, their cash flow is an essential component since they do not have the financial resources or financing leverage of larger firms. Faltering sales or lack of control over expenses opens such businesses to risks as a going concern. Therefore, timely reporting and discussions on current financial performance compared to budgets is a necessity for measuring operating and team performance and decisions. Informed brief performance status meetings keeps all team members abreast and knowledgeable of performance metrics, projects performance, and customer requirement issues as they arise.

Shared financial and nonfinancial data inform decision-making, and decision-making directs the business. If such data are not forthcoming at regular and close enough intervals, such a scenario can leave business decision-makers without critical information to manage the business and for holding the management team accountable for stated objectives and performance.

Once your company reaches month or quarter end and the results are in, the financial statements come under review for stakeholders. This chapter covers two basic ways of approaching review of the financial statements: vertical analysis and horizontal analysis, and both are equally useful.

Vertical Analysis

Vertical analysis enables you to evaluate performance on a periodic basis: monthly, quarterly, or annually. All three are highly preferred. Three measurements come into play in vertical analysis for identifying financial performance:

1. Percentage of a given base value
2. Financial ratios
3. The budget

The most common percentages of base value measurements for the income statement (see Figure 15.1) are gross margin and earnings before income tax (EBIT). These also act as financial objectives. The net sales number is the base denominator against which these financial performance numbers are measured.

	Period ended december 31,2014		% of income
Revenue	$ 12,986,320		100.0%
Cost of goods sold			
Direct materials	2,705,750		20.8%
Direct Labor	2,650,000		20.4%
Freight	158,700		1.2%
Other costs of goods sold	1,180,300		9.1%
Total cost of goods sold	6,694,750		51.6%
Gross profit	6,291,570		48.4%
Operating expenses			
Reasearch and development	1,400,000		10.8%
Sales and marketing	1,511,440		11.6%
General & administrative	3,474,605		
Business license & fees		44,100	0.3%
Automobile expenses		223,810	1.7%
Depreciation expenses		152,300	1.2%
Dues and subscriptions		36,200	0.3%
Insurance		355,200	2.7%
Facilities maintenance and repairs		151,850	1.2%
Small tools and equipment <1 year useful life		34,710	0.3%
Meals and entertainment		63,760	0.5%
Postage and delivery		62,190	0.5%
Professional fees		352,420	2.7%
Rent		470,050	3.6%
Supplies		357,780	2.8%
Telecommunications		310,030	2.4%
Utilities		246,005	1.9%
Travel		355,200	2.7%
Indirect salaries and wages		259,000	2.0%
Total operating expenses	6,386,045		49.2%
Operating income	(94,475)		-1.7%
Other income/expense			
Other income	44,547		0.3%
Other expense	(15,296)		-0.1%
Total other expense	29,251		0.2%
Net income	$ (65,224)		-0.5%

Figure 15.1. Sample percentage of value income statement.

The ratios of other expense categories, such as sales and other operating expense categories, are calculated accordingly. The percentage of value measurements for the income statement informs the executive team of the ratio of various expenses compared to net sales for determining if they are out of line compared to the budget (budget versus actual). This analysis will alert you about reasonable expenditures for each expense category.

For example, the income statement in Figure 15.1 highlights a negative net margin, indicating that expenditures are not in line with profit expectations, let alone with the company's targeted margin. An examination of the percentage of net revenue of specific line items will reveal which items exceed expectations for reasonableness. However, this cannot be fully determined until compared to budget.

The budget and financial ratios enter the picture as measurements at this point. Both of these are the tests for reasonableness. During the budget preparation process, your budget team established specific expenditures as reasonable for meeting your stated objectives, particularly gross and net profit. Financial ratios, especially as compared to industry averages, provide a benchmark for performance. Both the budget and industry financial ratios are internal and external benchmarks, respectively, that enable you to measure financial performance for each accounting period. For example, how do you know if your insurance costs are reasonable for your business size in your industry or for that matter sufficiently reasonable to meet your strategic goals? Aligning your budget, if it is financially feasible for the current budgeted period, with the industry average for your business size is a sound indicator. The industry average acts as a benchmark for insurance costs. Using industry benchmarks in establishing your budget gives you another key performance indicator (KPI) for determining if your expenses are reasonable.

All three financial statements come into view in the analysis of financial performance. This is especially true in the use of the three earlier-mentioned measurements: percentage method, ratios, and the budget. In applying the percentage method to the balance sheet, you can measure the ratio of particular assets or liabilities to total assets or liabilities to determine the weight any given asset carries compared to the others.

Consider the sample balance sheet in Figure 15.2. Notice that liquid cash (operating cash and marketable securities) comprises just 2.8% of total current assets. Trade receivables and inventories amount to 62.1% of total current assets. This weight places a serious strain on cash flow and inhibits the company from meeting its financial obligations reflected in its accounts payable. Inventories also reveal either slow sales or excess and obsolete inventory (E&O). The negative net income for the period that ends in December 31, 2014 confirms the build-up of inventories

	Period ended december 31,2014	%
ASSETS		
Cash	49,850	1.1%
Marketable securities	75,000	1.7%
Trade receivable	2,110,500	48.0%
Inventories	618,580	14.1%
Other current assets	70,000	1.6%
Total current assets	2,923,930	66.5%
Fixed assets		
Vehicels	235,000	5.3%
Plant & equipment	1,236,000	28.1%
Accumulated depreciation	(665,870)	-15.2%
Net fixed assets	1,471,000	33.5%
TOTAL ASSETS	4,394,930	100.0%
LIABILITIES & EQUITY		
Liabilities		
Current liabilities		
Accounts payable	1,611,000	36.7%
Line of credit	500,000	11.4%
Current portion of long-term debt	85,000	1.9%
Total current liabilities	2,196,000	50.0%
Long-term debt	2,000,000	45.5%
Total liabilities	4,196,000	95.5%
Equity		
Paid-in-capital	200,000	4.6%
Retained earnings	64,154	1.5%
Net income	(65,224)	-1.5%
Total equity	198,930	4.5%
TOTAL LIABILITIES & EQUITY	4,394,930	100.0%

Figure 15.2. Sample balance sheet showing percentage of value method.

Financial ratio formula	Ratio application
Current ratio–current assets/current liabilities	$2,923,930/$2,196,000 = 1.33
Acid test ratio–cash, marketable securities, and accounts receivable	$2,235,350/2,196,000 = 1.02
Cash ratio–cash and marketable securities	$ 134,850/2,196,000 = .06
Debt ratio–total liabilities/total assets	$4,196,000/4,394,930 = .95

Figure 15.3. The application of financial ratios to financial analysis.

resulting from slow sales. The percentage of value also reveals other contributing issues, such as the ratio of debt.

Financial ratios, to some degree give you similar results. However, reviewing the income statement and balance sheet from the view of the percentage method provides greater granularity by comparing any one-line items to a base value such as net revenues, total assets, or total liabilities. Doing this analysis is helpful in determining the soundness of a company's financial position. For example, consider the application of the Current Ratio to the balance sheet in Figure 15.3. The Current Ratio (1.33) is low enough to cause some alarm, compared to a 2.0 that an industry average may recommend.

However, this does not tell the entire story, because the Current Ratio does not consider the distribution of current assets in their respective accounts and the weight given to each. Therefore, by simply calculating the Current Ratio by itself, it would seem that there is not a deeply serious cash flow issue, although there is a cause of concern. The evaluation of this ratio also depends on the industry average. The Current Ratio does not highlight liquid cash (operating checking and convertible marketable securities).

While the percentage of a selected value (current or total assets) delves deeper to identify the overweight of trade receivables in the equation mix, another financial ratio confirms that liquidity is a looming problem that even the Acid Test or Quick Ratio overlooks. This ratio is the Cash Ratio. Compare the differences in Figure 15.3. The Cash Ratio reveals that available cash is dangerously below 1.0. This suggests a decline in cash over time and substantial cash weakness. This scenario indeed places the company in a serious cash situation for meeting its financial obligations, especially considering its debt leverage (Total Assets/Total Liabilities).

The level of accounts receivable compels a closer review for determining aged accounts beyond 30-, 60-, and 90-day past due payments or even if some may be uncollectable. A horizontal analysis (over several years) focusing on these accounts could reflect patterns. The high debt ratio reveals no financial flexibility and that the likelihood of assuming more debt to meet obligations or venturing into a new project is close to zero. Furthermore, if sales declined further, bankruptcy could be on the horizon.

Using financial ratios from industry averages aids in identifying how your company compares with peers or the competition. Industry financial ratios change from time to time to keep abreast with the changing financial conditions of companies in various industries. To stay informed about peers and competitors in your industry and for sound financial statements analysis, a subscription to firms that provide financial statement benchmarks would be highly useful. The Risk Management Association (RMA) is one of the major and highly respected firms that publish *The Annual Statement Studies: Financial Ratio Benchmarks* available to businesses for a subscription.

Horizontal Analysis

Horizontal analysis gives you a broader perspective of your financial performance and permits you to compare year over year, monthly, and quarterly performance trends. By using the same three measurements for vertical analysis, you can review the financial statements from the view of horizontal analysis. From a percentage of a given base value (e.g., net revenues), you can compare period financial statements across months, quarters, or years for determining historical financial performance over time. An aggregate comparison informs you of a trend in your financial condition, that is, if it is improving or deteriorating. A more detailed (by account) analysis can call your attention to useful information concerning some of the following financial issues and prompt strategic evaluation:

1. Expense trends from period to period (monthly and annually) for determining spikes in spending or spending levels on the rise, which could point to internal control issues

2. Management of specific assets or liabilities and how they fluctuate compared to other balance sheet or income statement values (e.g., accounts receivable or inventories with sales) and whether they require greater attention

3. Indication of weaknesses in financial condition that need attention or a change in business or financial strategy

4. Organizational issues that may need to be addressed, such as realignment or restructuring for greater efficiency, elimination of waste, or addressing the customer

5. Revenue trends that highlight customer management issues or market trends

6. Cost of goods sold issues that call for a more detailed analysis of materials costs, credit rating, or vendor selection

7. Inventory management issues that reveal the need to review process controls for some of the following:

   a. Cost reduction
   b. Work order management
   c. Improved production floor instructions
   d. Regular cycle counts
   e. Implementation of improved physical inventory procedures
   f. Excess and obsolescence review

8. Debt management issues that could highlight financial funding risks, credit rating, ability to meet financial obligations, cost of money, or cash flow stability

9. Customer management that lends to efficient collections and the prevention of write-offs of aged accounts

10. Banking management for testing the relationship and service level of financial institutions with which the company deals and how these constituents could foster improvements

When used in relation with external economic, marketing, or industry association trends and indicators (e.g., in comparison with producer price (PPI) or consumer price (CPI) indices, vendor performance, manufacturing new orders, or consumer expectations), you can determine if the external environment influenced specific areas of your financial performance, such as rising inventories or aging of vendor accounts. Such comparisons could lead to strategy updates and perhaps the formation of partnerships for corrective actions.

In addition, reviewing trade journals on economic activity in specific industries related to your customers or vendors could be insightful for your company's financial performance for gathering ideas on how to engage business performance issues at hand. This is a broad comparison, but such an analysis could prove useful if your business is sensitive to external drivers, such a fuel cost or scarce materials on which your business depends.

Financial ratios and your budget to actual comparisons can confirm the external influence on your financial performance. This is especially true if you use industry ratios for determining how you compare with other like businesses in your industry. If you have prior annual data that includes budget data, you can review how well you aligned with your budget over several years and pinpoint accounts with wide swings in variances from budget. Any wide variances from budget for specific line items on either your income statement or balance sheet could be indicators of internal control issues that would prompt a more detailed evaluation. For example, a rise in delinquent customer accounts could indicate an influence of troubling economic conditions that cause your customers to pay more slowly. This could also point to internal processes of accounts management, also. This could prompt a strategy for added incentives for early payments.

Monthly trends could also be an indicator of the need to evaluate specific process issues. For example, if warranty expenses increased over a several-month period and exhibited irregular spikes, is there a quality control issue during final product inspection? Another example is, did the forecast not anticipate product implementation labor requirements in a new location that recently started operations? An affirmation could drive a re-forecast and corrective action.

Such action keeps your company aligned not only with your stated goals but also with your competition who is bidding for your customers. By recognizing competitive financial positioning from the view of industry financial ratios, you can set your business on a stronger course.

You can also use industry financial ratio data as a standard for establishing improvement goals for strengthening your own financial position in comparison to industry averages. This is a proactive use of industry data for strategic and tactical purposes. Rather than simply using industry financial ratios to gauge how you compare to other companies in the industry, use it to strategize how you compete. Aiming at the upper quartile financially compared to industry financial standards fortifies your company to compete from strength. This in turn positions you for greater market penetration and holding to a set course during lean economic times.

Other Useful Metrics for Financial Review

Although vertical and horizontal analysis is a large segment of conducting a period-end financial review, other metrics come into view. These metrics serve to uncover financial performance measures that could prove highly useful that vertical and horizontal analyses do not consider. Setting these metrics up during budget preparation gives you additional targets for business performance. These metrics consist of the following:

1. Sales by customer—The sales by customer metric reveals brand loyalty, particularly given the number of purchases per customer. It can also reveal the attention a company gives to following up with and developing the customer.
2. Top 10 customer analysis—This metric examines the top 10 or 15 customers to determine if there a concentration of sales with these compared to total sales. Such an analysis could reflect revenue risk to your company. For example, if a few customers comprise a large amount of revenue and fail to return, this could cause a sizable decline in revenues and place your company at risk.
3. Sales by product—This metric reveals product performance compared to expectations and market research. It can provide insights into product market presence for determining actions to take for product disposition. Do they need to be retired from the product portfolio with new product offerings for replacements? Do they need new features or accessories? Are their price points reasonable? These and many other questions lend to product decision-making.
4. Sales by region or market segment—Which regions or markets are performing according to expectations? This metric addresses decisions concerning penetration, acceptance, growth, and saturation.

5. Sales by sales person—This metric gauges the productivity of sales personnel for compensation purposes.

6. Sales per employee—This metric gives insight into staff resources productivity and can determine the contribution of human resources to meeting stated objectives. Compared to the industry it can give a benchmark for the efficient use of resources.

Corrective Actions and Re-forecasts

The review of any one of the financial statements may prompt decisions concerning some of the following items or related issues:

1. Revenue shortfall or revenue performance not in keeping with strategic objectives for region, segment of the market, or product line

2. Gross margins that do not meet set goals

3. Alignment of actual expenses with budgets for a given category of expense

4. Cash flow and its impact on the ability of the company to meet financial obligations, to fund current operations, or to meet the need of budgeted new projects

5. High trade receivables with a set percentage having delinquent accounts (a metric should be established for days sales outstanding (DSO) and delinquent accounts for immediate action)

6. Debt leverage and progress toward relieving it and corresponding cost of money

7. Ongoing strategic direction based on budget to actual status review

Corrective Actions

Corrective actions are a response primarily to adverse findings from the periodic review of financial statements. This is why review intervals are important. Monthly reviews give you an opportunity to tackle negative performance or to response to more positive market or economic conditions. Missed opportunity or declining performance could arise when financial review intervals are farther apart. Corrective action could also result from discovery of greater than expected performance from the financial review. A course correction in this case may call for greater aggressiveness in the market to take advantage of opportunity.

Corrective action considers not only the review of financial metrics but also analysis of nonfinancial metrics. These metrics relate to those the budget team established for organizational and process improvements and for implementation of best practices as discussed in the previous section of this chapter. The following checklist provides an approach to determine their impact on your overall business strategy and corresponding objectives:

1. Review the income statement to determine significant variances from stated objectives, specifically revenue, gross margin, net income, or balance sheet items or cash flow.
2. Is there a trend for the variances or can you make some minor adjustments to make up for any negative costs variance?
3. Review existing projects to determine if their completion is in jeopardy due to any costs variances. For example, you may have a project for opening a new warranty service office or for distribution of products in another geographical location. Are you significantly over budget for staying on course? Do you need to adjust the timeline? What impact will this have on market opportunity, lost revenue, or cash flow? If the project is a multiyear endeavor (such as the implementation of a financial management or information technology system), how will the variances impact outlying years?
4. Do project slips influence the accomplishment of strategic objectives?
5. Is there a need to reconsider vendor performance due to higher than standard cost variances?
6. Will you need to adjust objective timeline by extending it out farther, adjust costs for completing the objective, or consider adjustments to objective or strategy?
7. For a positive variance, can you shift funds to other projects that may be showing a negative variance without a negative impact in objectives?
8. Can you take advantage of a market opportunity with a significant positive variance that may be advantageous to the company?

9. Would you prefer to be conservative and place costs savings in a reserve for future use?

10. Is the cost variance due to a process weakness that needs adjusting or modifying? What needs to be done to correct this?

11. Do variances require greater oversight of processes or projects for the remainder of the budget period?

12. Was your budget too optimistic?

These inquiries and questions are by no means comprehensive, but they will provide you an analytical methodology for getting to the root of any issues related to any one of your financial statements. Any one of the above items in the checklist may require a decision for re-forecasting financial performance.

Contingent Planning, Adaptation, and Re-forecasting

Contingent planning is considering alternative decisions if a given course of action turns negative or if opportunity presents itself. Contingency is a worthy practice for navigating a fast-paced marketplace or volatile economic conditions. It is a continuous planning process for staying one step ahead of the competition and for reading the external environment. This process seeks to scale the company's reach from the readings it receives from financial data, customer demand, competition, available resources, and economic conditions. This process suggests taking advantage of adaptive forecasts and making adjustments internally in response to the external environment. Markets and the economy change rapidly, and a company needs to be sufficiently flexible to address them.

Nokia saw the need to adopt a contingency planning methodology for addressing competition from Microsoft.[2] Its response to any success with Microsoft and its impact on Nokia's market share meant a Plan B for the company. This meant responding quickly with costs allocation when feasible to adapt to a different strategy for other revenue streams. Nokia saw that this is what it took to thrive in the market. Tim Berry writes, "Business planning is about managing change."[3] Nokia weighed the cost to change against strategic opportunity. The same goes for budgeting as a planning practice. The five issues he addresses that are applicable to this discussion consist of

1. the imminence of change;
2. managing change;
3. making assumptions;
4. having more than one plan; and
5. planning is better than not planning.

These five points speak of contingency and align with Nokia's philosophy.

While target numbers for revenues, expenses, and capital outlays give direction and focus, having built-in flexibility to navigate change provides for a soft landing or success when markets change or the economy goes south. Flexibility not only makes you ready for negative news but also for positive outcomes. However, such flexibility can encounter existing commitments, such as retooling, for taking another strategic direction. Such commitments call for weighing any shift in direction and the costs associated with such a shift. Therefore, it is a good idea to have a cost–benefit analysis for a Plan B on the table for financial and business performance reviews in responding to market, economic, or competitive variables such as those that Nokia encountered with Microsoft.

David Anderson cites Peter Drucker as a pioneer with the adaptive framework.[4] His argument from Drucker is that in the knowledge worker economy, a plan-driven process falls into obsolescence in modern markets and economic conditions in which innovation and intense competition trumps a plan set in stone. I would modify that argument somewhat. Do not forego planning with a budget as Tim Berry suggests, but be ready to adapt to current conditions. This means that collaboration and communication within a flat organization allows for a faster response to market and economic conditions. In addition, the financial plan as defined in the budget must be flexible, while still providing direction and targets.

The Rolling Forecast

Frequently, a one-year revenue budget rapidly becomes out of date due to market and economic uncertainties and the need for a rapid response to them and the competition. Many who oppose the annual budget scenario perceive it as locking them into a straightjacket or a static forecast.[5] Market, economic, and competitive variables require a methodology that provides a more rapid response to them. The rolling forecast offers that methodology with any modifications to it you need to accommodate to your business. Adopting a rule wholesale can also produce a straightjacket. Innovation in planning is just as important as innovation in product development.

Many small-to-medium-sized business accounting software applications have both a budget and re-forecast module in them. If they do not, third-party applications compatible with the accounting system can be integrated with it. With them, businesses can set up a budget for several years for all three financial statements. They can also develop a forecast for up to 12 months based on cash flow variables and response to positive or negative external forces and opportunities.

This book proposes that the budget is a targeting mechanism established through objectives from a strategic plan. However, objective setting is only as good as the underlying market, economic, and competitive data and the resources required to meet them. If markets or the economy changes, this may lead to a modification of objectives. Sometimes, these conditions call for adjustments to respond faster to targeted objectives or adjusting objectives to capitalize on shifting economic or market challenges or opportunities.

The rolling forecast can be integrated into an annual budget plan tied to the accounting system and provide a means of quickly adapting to changing variables in the external environment. While the annual budget captures and tracks targets, the rolling forecast gives updates and releases a company from a strict stand-alone annual budget format while maintaining the original budget numbers. Quarterly updates are preferable since lead times for projects in many manufacturing companies frequently exceed a month. Companies in some industries, such as internet-based one, may need a rolling forecast on a monthly basis because of rapid changes occurring in those industries.

Many corporate planners view the rolling forecast as a continuous adjustment and never look back to original numbers or what they refer to as a static budget.[6] Rather external and internal conditions change future revenue streams and costs. The plan must then change to accommodate these conditions. Still, smaller companies either do not budget at all or cannot afford the price for more sophisticated planning tools that include rolling forecasts or re-forecast methods. Consequently, they remain with the traditional budget approach, using separate applications from the accounting system for adjusting forecasts.

Although this book takes the annual budget approach, the author suggests an accommodation principle. That is, consider the outline of the budget process suggested in this book, and revisit objectives and budgeted forecasts quarterly using a project approach. For example, if an opportunity arises through a new or existing channel, partnership, or joint venture for greater sales, budget team members derive a business plan to address the opportunity. In preparing a business plan to address opportunity, consider the following steps:

1. Identify the opportunity.
2. Review the long-term effect of the opportunity in terms of return on investment, market penetration, or other factors related to your business.
3. Draft a set of objectives and corresponding adjusting forecast to sales, expenses, and capital outlays.
4. Review existing commitments for determining short-term and long-term cost or revenue impact from the perspective of the new opportunity or the need to shift course.
5. Retain what remains unchanged in the original budget while defining the project's tasks, resources, revenue, and costs.
6. Draft a project implementation plan to respond to the opportunity or new course shift.

Working with Finance, team members can prepare a pro forma cash flow alongside a pro forma income statement for the project initiative. Such an approach allows for rapid deployment of initiatives as they surface with a bottom-up planning response approach. The same action could occur in response to any other changing market or economic variables influencing your company's original budget. Such initiatives respond to immediate events occurring during a given month or quarter.

Any budget team member initiating such an event or recognizing market, competitive, or economic changes can raise the issue or challenge prior to any quarter end. Consequently, they would have gained the buy-in and be working on any revenue (with corresponding expenses) or capital project prior to any quarter forecast. At the quarter-end financial and business performance review, the budget team member would be prepared to review existing actions and opportunities. All team members would also be on board. Therefore, they are already prepared to provide any rolling re-forecast with a high degree of certainty.

Steven Bragg has a similar term for such a scenario—"recasting of the budget."[7] This principle is not too far removed from the rolling forecast as a total replacement for the budget especially for the smaller business attempting to stay abreast with the market with funding constraints. Rather, it is a modified approach with built-in flexibility for a rapid response to market opportunity or new competitive information.

APPENDIX A

Suggested Budget Process Task List

If you currently do not have a budget process, the one in Table A.1 below can provide you with a template guide. Add or modify it according to your company requirements.

Table A.1. Budget Process Task List (see the Microsoft Excel Business Budget Builder)

Sample responsibility legend CEO—CEO/President, CFO—CFO, TM—Team Manager (includes all participants)		
Task	Responsible	Date
STAGE I [Start date: _____ Completion date: _____]		
Team selection and kick-off meeting agenda		
Kick-off meeting agenda disseminated prior to kick-off meeting		
Organizational structure integrity review		
Outsourcing review: vendor qualification, selection, and contractual agreements updates		
Organizational chart update and reflection of outsourcing		
KMA identification and managerial chart development		
Processes reviews and updates		
Internal controls and risks exposure review		
Historical and current funding requirements review and ratios analyses		
Preliminary sales forecast		
STAGE II [Start Date: _____ Completion Date: _____]		
Objectives development		
Performance review criteria and scoring development		
Budget assumptions		
The baseline and historical financial statements review		

(*Continued*)

STAGE II [Start Date: _____ Completion Date: _____]		
Budget project scheduling and deadlines		
Sales Plan		
Baseline sales definition		
Objectives, performance measurement, and performance criteria		
Products overview and positioning		
Industry analysis		
Markets definition and size		
Customer profiles		
Marketing plan		
Advertising plan		
Partnerships and joint ventures plan		
Sales budget for existing markets		
Sales budget for new markets		
Sales budget for existing products		
Sales budget for new products		
Sales budget for existing channels		
Sales budget for new channels		
Pricing strategy		
Sales roll-up		
Capital plan—see Chapter 8		
Market opportunities review for capital assets support		
Identification of projects in support of marketing opportunities		
Current facilities and capital equipment review for supporting sales and marketing plan		
Identification of assets replacement, replacement costs, and impact on income statement for tax purposes, cash flow, and profit		
Identification of new capital purchases, facilities, and tenant improvements		
Financial management capital requirements		
Information technology capital requirements for customer efforts and support		
Manufacturing and production capital requirements		
Marketing and sales campaign and sales equipment and software applications		
Research and development capital requirements		
Asset purchase calendar		

STAGE II [Start Date: _____ Completion Date: _____]		
Internal operations versus outsourcing		
Manufacturing Plan		
Manufacturing and facilities layout		
Warehousing and inventory management		
Machinery maintenance, upgrades, and installation		
Office space for production support		
Shop floor management		
Capacity planning management		
Purchasing management		
Vendor management		
Standards management		
Documentation control management		
Configuration management		
Engineering change control management		
Product project management controls		
Material requirements planning		
Administrative Plan		
IT and communications		
Facilities requirements and management		
Insurance coverage		
Transportation and travel		
Accounting and legal		
Repairs and maintenance		
Small tools, equipment, and supplies		
Total Staffing Plan Roll-up		
Full-time Equivalent (FTE) headcount, part-time, and temporary staffing		
Base compensation roll-up		
Job descriptions		
Objectives and performance measurements		
Cross training and work coverage		
Costs burden (taxes, benefits, insurances)		
Records management		
Payroll management		
Pro forma financial statements preparation and ratios		

(Continued)

STAGE III [Start Date: _____ Completion Date: _____]		
Execution plan		
Status meeting schedule		
Status meeting agenda development		
Metrics		
Performance measurements and benchmarks development		
Reporting		
Training and orientation		

APPENDIX B

Customer Management Best Practices

Among the most important constituent that drives the company is the customer. According to Drucker, the customer is the reason for the company's existence. Customers are your primary constituent, so spend time at the front end preparing a sound management plan for them. Their managing takes a high priority.

A number of useful guidelines will help you better manage the customer for ensuring customer retention and improving communications between your company and the customer. Implementing these guidelines during the budget process sets expectations from the beginning. They will help you protect your revenue stream from competitors, ensure effective cash flow, and give your customers confidence in your ability to deliver on their behalf. Among these guidelines are the following:

- Customer Credit Checks and Ratings
- Agreements and Terms
- Records Management
- Relationship Management
- Customer Benchmarking

These items obviously do not comprise an exhaustive list of guidelines. However, they are best practice areas that extend your reach with the customer for fostering a long and loyal relationship.

Customer Credit Checks and Ratings

Company's who do not conduct credit checks on their customers heighten risks to revenue and cash flow. This happens in both a business-to-business relationship as well as a business-to-consumer one. There is costs related to checking a customer's credit, but the benefit of doing so far outweighs the costs. For example, if you have a current bad debt ratio of 4% with an annual revenue stream of $12 million, you are losing cash receipts of $480,000. Compare this to a credit check subscription of $200–$400 annually. This amounts to pennies of prevention compared to a risks of substantial loss. If you do not have a credit monitoring subscription with one of the credit agencies, the budget is the place to put one in place.

How does obtaining a customer's credit check and ratings go toward fostering a sound relationship with a customer? Consider the following reasons:

1. It sets expectations and communicates to the customer that you take the customer relationship seriously.
2. It informs you about the customer's willingness to do business with you by having its own financial house in order. A peer relationship exhibits willingness and readiness to do business.
3. There is an implied willingness on the part of both parties to see the other succeed.

Credit rating agencies monitor the credit of almost all businesses throughout the United States and internationally. They produce credit reports much like those for individuals. However, ratings for businesses differ from those for individuals. Obtaining a credit report on a customer will reduce the risk to cash flow and added expense. It also informs you of the customer's ability to pay and credit worthiness.

Doing business with confidence and without interruption, due to bad credit, is a first start in creating sound business relationships. Writing off bad debt incurs far more expense than the costs of a credit monitoring subscription. You may wish to review historical bad debt write-offs for your budget forecast and set a target for bad debt and aging of accounts.

Agreements and Terms

Having a well-written contract agreement with your customers sets expectations and understanding between you and them. Often in manufacturing, retail, and wholesale, the purchase order acts as an agreement.

However, it may serve the purpose of a single transaction unless it is a blanket purchase order. It may also fail to spell out all terms and conditions. With some customers, you may want to identify detailed terms for delivery, returns, performance, timeliness, quality, issues elevation, insurance coverage, and related issues. This detailed agreement acts as the business partner agreement, whereas the purchase order is the individual transaction, project, or job agreement.

Both are best practices for establishing a clear and sound business relationship. The budget process is the place and time for reviewing and updating current agreements and for establishing new ones. Doing so prevents surprises and reduces risks to business transactions and your own business performance on behalf of your customer.

During the budget cycle, include as one of your activities a review of current contracts and agreements. You may wish to obtain contract or agreement templates or software applications that cover pertinent terms and conditions, warranties, liability coverage, and other related issues relative to your products or services. By using a template, you save time and money, and you are able to include all necessary terms with your customer. Obtaining or retaining legal expertise for reviewing agreements is another best practice. Such legal oversight can prevent the higher costs of future legal retention.

Records Management

Setting up and maintaining a sound records management system establishes an efficient audit trail for your customer and vendor transactions, a sound foundation for financial reporting, and a clear path for filing tax returns. Effective records management helps resolve disputes with your customers and vendors for reducing legal action. Sound records management serves as effective internal controls and lends to accuracy of the financial statements.

As part of information and communications segments of the business, having all the elements of records management provide you with the ability to

1. validate customer transactions;
2. monitor terms compliance;

3. record financial transactions in the proper period; and

4. maintain open communications with your customer on product and service delivery and corresponding timely fulfillment of their financial obligations.

The budget cycle gives you the opportunity to review records management systems for determining any required updates for adequately recording, reporting, and monitoring transactions with customers. Some questions for answering during this review are the following:

1. Is there any risk exposure in our records management systems?
2. Do our practices close risk gaps?
3. Do we need to tighten our processes for ensuring misreporting, reducing risks to revenues, and negatively influencing cash flow?

Omitting best practice documentation methods leaves a company open to liability. Many exclude or neglect such practices because they consider them as time-consuming, burdensome, and unwieldy. Most neglected practices consist of

1. no sales order or work order (or similar agreements) that gives the go ahead and instructions for customer purchase;
2. no relationship between the customer purchase order and internal sales or work order;
3. no method for returns or refunds;
4. poor cash handling so that the payment amount may not reach accounting for proper recording against invoices. This also applies to electronic funds transfers and related online transactions by debit or credit cards or e-checks;
5. an accounting system that does not accommodate certain critical features in the customer management process. This may include a customer relationship management (CRM) application not capable of integrating with the accounting system; and
6. a weak mechanism for follow up on collections for maintaining budgeted optimal cash flow.

The budget cycle is the best time to review the entire customer management cycle for ensuring that such gaps and corresponding risks have solutions.

Relationship Management

Marketing, continued sales, product and service delivery, and customer satisfaction depend on maintaining accurate and up-to-date information on customers. Marketing activity to prospects for filling the sales pipeline depend on relationship management practices.

There are a number of good CRM applications for capitalizing on improving this practice. Obtaining one that can integrate with your accounting system will make this practice much more efficient and accurate in updating customer records for selling, service, and customer management. Including this activity in the budget cycle allows you to assess the reliability of your current methods and applications and determine the cost benefit of improving on them.

Customer Benchmarks

Benchmarking measures the effectiveness of a given process, activity, or the financial condition of your company compared to certain internal and external measurements. Having designed benchmarks during the budget cycle allows you to measure targets effectiveness when they arise. Given the customer is a major constituent, measuring company performance related to the customer provides a mechanism of how well your company performs. This is a critical part of customer retention.

There are several ways of benchmarking customers for company performance on their behalf. Three major ones consist of the following:

1. Review of historical data
2. Establishment of internal benchmarks
3. Using industry benchmarks

There are a number of benchmarks related to customer management. However, this section highlights four major ones:

1. Customer service
2. Customer satisfaction
3. Competitive benchmarks
4. Financial performance related to customer management

Why Establish Benchmarks for the Customer?

This book concerns customer-driven budgeting. As such, benchmarking becomes a way to make budgeting customer driven. Benchmarks are metrics, standards, and performance criteria for measuring business performance against specific targets. Since the customer drives business, one of the first places to start is with benchmarking customer activity. How does a company gauge its success in the markets? Benchmarks answer this question.

Designing and Creating Benchmarks

Customer services is a very broad term, almost making benchmarking nuanced or highly customizable when seeking industry benchmarks. Customer satisfaction may appear too vague and requires definition. Competitive benchmarks may be difficult to obtain. What is the particular service, and are there sufficient data for deriving an adequate industry benchmark? How do you define satisfaction? Another difficulty arises when seeking an industry standard for benchmarks is identifying similar size companies that have a comparable service and then identifying the leader or leaders.

Eric Harmon, Schott Hensel, and Tim Lukes from McKinsey & Co. highlight several issues with customer services benchmarking.[1] First, services are far more difficult to benchmark than manufacturing processes (or for that matter any business process). The number of variables involved, especially considering people, makes for a less controlled environment for establishing strict benchmarks. Second, the services themselves are different. They write,

> The more types of services a business offers the more variability it can expect in its agreements. The metrics for a help desk that provides customer support for 5,000 users in a 9-to-5 office are very different from those for a help desk that supports logistics in a round-the-clock industrial environment. Even when offerings are similar, variances can be introduced locally through the way contracts are interpreted.[2]

Third, the business environment, equipment, and the overall infrastructure vary widely from company to company in the same industry.

Consequently, the variables for measurement make it difficult to establish true benchmarks. Fourth, even in the same industry for similar size companies, work volume lends to greater variances that impede solid benchmarking.

What then are some solutions for benchmarking customer services, satisfaction, and competition? The authors suggest that while peer benchmarks could be useful, they are just ballpark samples. Consequently, they suggest several approaches:

- Internal benchmarks
- Measuring cost drivers
- Measuring in depth and widely[3]

Internal benchmarks measure against actual achievement and reality. Being internal, you can be more proactive in establishing them and in measuring their success. There would also be no need for translating and scaling the metrics of external benchmarks for use internally. When combined with cost drivers, the authors contend that companies can discover underlying causes hindering performance and set up measurements for improvement.[4] Resources may make comprehensive measurements prohibitive although such an approach would lead to greater efficiency and cost reduction.

Action Item: Implementing Customer Management Best Practices

For implementing customer management best practices over time, consider a multistep process over a longer period. What can you do now? What can wait? During the budget kick-off meeting, ensure that customer management best practices are high on the agenda. Set up the best practices you want to target (such as projects) with the following 10 milestones:

1. Gain a buy-in from budget team members.
2. Appoint a champion for identifying areas for best practices.
3. Outline benchmark benefits for customer retention.
4. Conduct research on the type of best practices you want to establish.
5. Set targets so there will be measurements criteria.

6. Identify the tools you need for data collection and reporting.
7. Identify resources requirements (human, material, capital, and supplies).
8. Develop a scorecard and conduct performance reviews.
9. Set up a monitoring system.
10. Set your return on investment (ROI) target.

Two key elements in establishing customer services best practices are communication and targets. Communicating with your team and gaining their buy-in first multiplies your champions and success factor. This action also builds support for best practices. Make the goal clear: customer attainment and retention. Create a project team (no more than three people depending on the size of your company) for meeting and designing the selected best practices according to the milestones above. Involve the team in drafting an implementation plan with a go-live date. The final milestone of ROI is critical for implementation. Having a member of Finance on the team will provide you with the numbers side and modeling capability for ROI. In addition, Finance can add value to the financial performance (ratios) side of customer management best practices.

Major Vendor Management Best Practices and Policies

Vendor management places you in the driver's seat and provides a competitive edge with exercise over quality, innovation, pricing, and customer delivery. Vendor evaluation and selection is essential for effective budget management and maximizing growth and profits. Vendor management ensures successful performance in your business supply chain. Certain best practices will allow you to establish effective and efficient processes to curtail costs, obtain timely delivery of goods and services, ensure quality, and manage optimal terms.

Outsourcing Practices

Outsourcing is an essential part of reducing costs and improving productivity. Conducting evaluations of your vendors during the budget cycle and intervals in between give you the advantage of a full vendor review and reduces mid-course corrections when vendors fail to meet expectations. It also permits you to

1. perform those activities you do best;
2. concentrate on your core competencies;
3. rely on the expertise of outside sources that provide products and services more effectively for their delivery; and
4. create a competitive edge for your business.

Vendor selection serves three major arrangements for the business:

1. Product materials and subassemblies sourcing and multisourcing
2. Product-related contract services, such as delivery, installation, implementation services, technical support, and warranty services

3. Outsourced organizational components: services related to business administration, such as telecommunications services, utilities, website development and maintenance, payroll preparation, and various professional services (legal and tax planning and preparation)

Sometimes you will be limited in cost reduction for outsourced organizational components, such as for telecommunications. However, this does not mean that such a review is not necessary. The review may uncover unneeded services or offered available discounts made available to businesses like yours.

The budget cycle is one of the best times to perform an evaluation of existing vendor contracts and agreements. Such an evaluation could determine if vendors provide a competitive advantage, are cost effective, support your supply chain, and offer you the products and services you require for managing your business. However, to maintain a competitive edge, outsourcing and multisourcing are continuous tasks, with assessments occurring during the entire budget cycle.

It is easy to overlook some areas of outsourcing when overshadowed by those areas considered more important, such as production. While production vendor sourcing relates directly to the customer, it would be a detriment to minimize other areas. This discussion treats three distinct outsourcing components:

1. Product development and production
2. Contract services
3. Outsourced organizational components

By treating them distinctly, you will not overlook them during the budget cycle or during the course of the fiscal year.

Product Development and Production Sourcing

The key to cost-effective product or services development is the implementation of a systematic multisourcing plan as applicable to your business. Vendor multisourcing reduces costs and risks, while increasing a competitive advantage and quality. When your vendors realize they are bidding for your services through multisourcing arrangements, they will supply you with sourcing solutions that tend to reduce your risks with competitive expertise while being more transparent with their own price points and support. That is, multisourcing causes vendors to rise to the occasion with quality and price performance.

Often the reason for outsourcing in the first place is to seek an expert solution not readily available internally for meeting stated costs objectives and resource requirements. Most companies do not have all the expertise, because that would be cost-prohibitive. Consequently, outsourcing offers a preferred answer for product or service delivery when internal solutions are not feasible. While this may be true, you will still need a means for judging the quality of the products or services you receive for a competitive price point. Quality and price delivery points to having sound criteria for evaluating vendor selection. However, having criteria alone is insufficient for a solid outsourcing plan.

Anna Frazzetto offers 10 tips for successful outsourcing. Although her tips are from an IT perspective and a recruiter for IT talent, these 10 tips can apply to any situation whether IT or product development. They provide a sound checklist for anyone preparing an outsourcing plan.[1] Among the most valuable ones related to product development include the following strategies:

1. A strong internal support team
2. Standardization across selected vendors
3. Due diligence in pursuing the best vendors
4. Proper governance and risk reduction
5. The establishment of measurements

Frazzetto's article and subsequent question and answer discussion associated with a webinar she hosted is a valuable source for any company considering outsourcing and especially multisourcing.[2] In it, she examines all important issues of relationship building, geography, differentiation, process improvement, and overhead costs, all necessary ingredients of successful outsourcing. Depending on your company size, these issues can make or break your company's ability to deliver to the customer. Dean Davison highlights 10 risks involved in offshore outsourcing to which a company to international trade should pay close attention:[3]

1. Cost reduction expectations
2. Data security/protection that considers vendor security practices and intellectual property protection
3. Process discipline and associated cost savings with such discipline oversight
4. Loss of business knowledge and gaps that could lend to compromise
5. Vendor failure to deliver and contingency planning related to supplier delivery
6. Scope creep (change orders) and the cost management of outsourced contracts
7. Government oversight or regulation and compliance and transparency in light of international trade laws and regulations
8. Culture and training for ensuring consistency in service delivery
9. Turnover of personnel and liability reduction in outsourced staffing
10. Knowledge transfer and it management

These risk factors can serve as a checklist for developing an outsourcing plan and expenses associated with them. These expenses can then be weighed against costs and benefits related to supplier outsourcing.

Due diligence associated with all areas of vendor performance can make a huge difference with selection. Within the context of international trade and the risks and legal concerns associated with it, it is important not to neglect requirements related to import or export business. Businesses thrive in a world economy and thereby forced to deal with all the variables and challenges associated with it.

William Poe identifies a number of issues facing import or export transactions: "organizational structure, taxes, insurance, financing, payment, and customer."[4] He also identifies the various international and United States federal entities with which a company will need to interact for conducting international business transactions. In light of these two factors, Poe recommends a checklist to get through the regulatory gauntlet for international trade. The criteria outlined under the topic of *Administrative Outsourcing* below also have a high degree of relevance to product development.

Contract Services

Although different in terms of type of vendors used, contract or subcontract services are equally as important for outsourcing. Postproduct release and delivery call for their support in the field or office. Warranty and technical support concerning the products set up, use, troubleshooting, repair, or replacements are as much a part of the product and supply chain as the product itself. Given the complexity and dependencies of supporting a myriad of products in a high technology environment worldwide, warranty management must keep up to deliver value to customers. Warranty management can be a make or break situation for your company's retention of customers. There are a number of decision points in the warranty chain that a company must consider in the delivery and support of products.

James Taylor, CEO of Decision Management Solutions, suggests a decision tree for providing "the biggest pay-off for the warranty process" that includes items like warranty claims, problem identification, and parts service.[5] He also suggests best practices for tightening warranty delivery that include constant improvement, fraud detection, and simplification of the warranty process. A company must consider not only the budgeted costs of warranty improvements but also the returns in terms of cost reduction and customer retention versus the cost of business by not applying best practices to warranty chain management. Taylor suggests that a "decision-centric" (decision tree) approach can lead to the desired improvements in warranty delivery.[6] This in turn provides for costs reduction and customer retention. This scenario holds true for product technical support, an ancillary service for warranties.

If you do not currently have the resources to provide technical or warranty support or it is cheaper to outsource it, the infrastructure for doing so requires careful planning. Making the right selections for such support leads to a long-term relationship with your customer or the customer seeking another product. Therefore, outsourcing for contract services cannot be overlooked in the professional services budget.

Outsourced Organizational Components

Administrative outsourcing sometimes leaves business owners distant from managing the full organization. They must accommodate for this distant management when considering outsourcing critical management functions, such as accounting or IT. Time delays in outsourced services could be more costly than their actual expense if they have insufficient oversight.

David Borowski of Pace Harmon Consultancy suggests a checklist of 10 items that eases outsourcing. The more prominent ones are transition costs, evaluation criteria, communication, encouragement of innovation, tough negotiations, and service level agreements.[7] The checklist he provides is a good start for thinking through outsourcing solutions. However, there are a number of variables to consider when planning outsourcing of a business component.

Poor responsiveness from outside vendors or an ill-defined scope of work for the vendor can be distractive. One distraction is not having sufficient knowledge when needed for sound decision-making. This lack can lead to delays and added expenses. When these distractions set in, the one entity that really has the highest priority takes a setback: customer management. Often, these distractions seem unavoidable with a growing business when attempting to push through to the next revenue goal on limited internal resources. However, laying the groundwork by preparing an organizational chart like the one shown in Figure C.1 can lessen distractions. This business model clarifies and makes visible outsourced components of the organization directly on the organization chart.

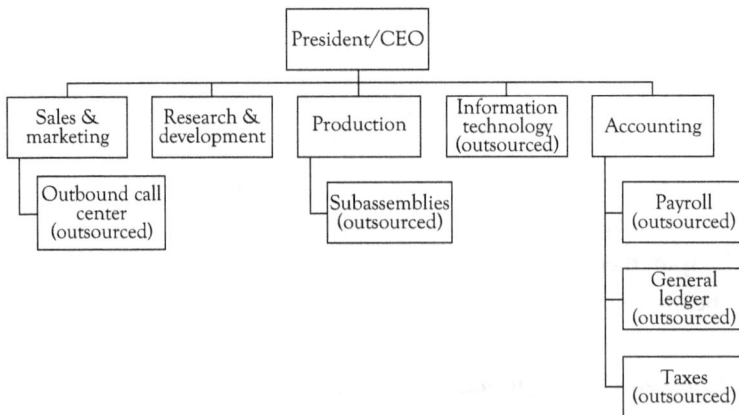

Figure C.1. The organization showing internal and outsourced functions.

This organizational chart recognizes the outsourced components of the business and treats them like all other functions. They perform work, meet performance criteria, and report on activities just like internal ones. If the company neglects to recognize outsourced business components like those internally, it could

- fail to account for all the resources to manage it in the budget;
- neglect to show it as part of its organization and its incorporation into total business efforts;
- underestimate its value and contribution to the company;
- not account for criteria for and reporting on performance in a service contract;
- not exercise proper safeguards over company assets and disclosure of confidential and sensitive data for the outsourced portion of the business;
- not provide for a full set of tasks or duties the outsourced vendor performs for the function; and
- not having it customer-centered.

Administrative Outsourcing

Administrative outsourcing can be pushed to the bottom of the outsourcing list in importance. In doing so, administrative costs can easily spin out of control if agreements for them do not hold equal weight as other supplier outsourcing. Some of the more prominent administrative outsourced components are payroll, legal, public relations, financial institutions, advertising, collections, and tax preparation. Each industry that these vendors represent has a large number of firms that specialize or offer a full array of services associated with each profession. Would you also need services at a future date in another area that a speciality firm does not offer? This question could also factor into your selection decision.

Before signing on the dotted line for any one of them, wisdom dictates interviewing your selection for their strengths and reputation. In addition, ask for available references regarding their work. Review any agreement carefully to ensure that it fits your criteria list and score the criteria to determine if the vendor would be a best fit for your culture and customer. While they may not deal directly with your customer, they do offer indirect support. How they interact with you will determine how they champion your customers. Assigning responsibility over each outsourced area gives you greater grasp in managing all vendors and their respective costs. Their management can have tax implications.

Ensure that any agreement you sign releases you from statutory control over how they work for you. A point of contact within your company gives you the assurance that outsourced firms or professionals deliver according to agreements and gives you leverage over costs, guarantees, and products and services.

The concept of the *lean* organization lends to streamlining so that outsourcing is much more common than in previous decades. Because of the increased frequency of outsourcing, companies may be tempted to leave managing the outsourced components of the business to the vendor. This tends to outsource responsibility and accountability, also. Outsourcing responsibility and accountability in their entirety can create a breakdown in safeguards. The organizational reporting structure in Figure B.1 ensures that the firm does not overlook outsourced business components in the budget or fail to recognize it as an integrated and important part of the organization.

When outsourcing business components, it is important that the company establish a sound agreement with the vendor. The contractual arrangement with the outsourced vendor should reflect work performance, reporting requirements, and the negotiated compensation for the work performed. These criteria ensure that the vendor assumes certain responsibility and corresponding accountability.

You also need to establish disclosure agreements and lay the groundwork for other contractual issues. Take care to ensure that contractual arrangements comply with Internal Revenue Service (IRS) conditions of not exercising control and for reporting for tax purposes (IRS form 1099).[8] The arrangement falls under the purview of vendor management. The set-aside budget is the entire liability amount for the outsourced business component. Identify specific criteria for the vendor to ensure that outsourced business components are fully integrated into the company. Table C.1 gives a checklist that offers a sample of such criteria. Write such criteria into the vendor service contract.

Table C.1. Outsourcing Vendor Criteria

Outsourcing vendor criteria
1. Define its scope of work as though it were part of internal operations.
2. Ensure the outsourced vendor covers such works that the company will not be performing.
3. Specify with vendor and employees how it fits in the organization and processes.
4. Identify vendor management for escalating issues with vendor services or products.
5. Define products or services warranties management corresponding terms and conditions.
6. Define scheduling and availability requirements. These requirements include lead-time for material, equipment, or service deliveries as needed.
7. Research the vendor's record of accomplishment with other companies. Obtain at least three references.
8. Determine performance criteria for the outsourced vendor, including reporting, objectives, deliverables, and periods for meeting these criteria.
9. Ensure that vendors have licensing and certifications as required for the performance of the outsourced function. These qualifications could include "green" technology requirements and certifications.
10. Ask for references to determine how well the vendor has performed for others.
11. Verify supplier liability insurance for risk reduction in supplies and services delivery.
12. Have the vendor sign a code of conduct that complies with internal business practices. Most states have business and professions codes that define business behavior and transactions. Review this business and professions code for applicability to the vendor.
13. Have the vendor sign a nondisclosure agreement related to company confidential and sensitive information.
14. Provide the vendor with company internal operating procedures and specifications related to outsourced activities and standards for meeting quality assurance.
15. Ensure that the performance contract complies with IRS rules concerning independent contractors.
16. Define terms of payment.

Prior to issuing the contract, evaluate the length of time for outsourcing the function before staffing it internally. Perform a cost–benefit analysis to determine which would be better: internal staffing or outsourcing the function. When a vendor (rather than employees) assumes responsibilities for an entire business component (such as IT), that vendor often becomes simply one of many the firm uses for materials, services, and equipment. By incorporating it into the organization chart as an outsourced component, the company does not neglect it and raises its importance to the company. When the time comes for bringing the business component internally, the company will already have the performance requirements for it defined for making a handoff to internal management and staff that will perform the work.

Conclusion

There is a continuous cycle in almost all events. The economy and markets drive business cycles in what appears to be a chaotic manner. However, there are deliberation, focus, decision-making, and constant movement within one firm and another as they trade, negotiate, set terms in contracts, and create value and wealth for a multitude of stockholders. From a distance, what seems random is calculated and purposeful. In a televised interview, Steve Forbes once said, "The markets like it messy."

Companies strive to get ahead as they engage is business development, creating, selling, buying, and making their mark on producing products and services for giving consumers what they want and satisfying their demands. This is messy business. Many businesses start and crash. Others continue on meeting their targets earning value for themselves and their constituents.

This fluctuation in the marketplace is the typical business cycle that in turn creates a life cycle of products and services through invention and innovation. Product life cycles take consumers on a winding ride toward increasing technological advance from harnessing raw materials and creating them into finished products.

What is the difference between finishers and failures? Tenacity? Grit? Intelligence? An idea brought to fruition? All businesses have these qualities in varying degrees, but many still fail. I hope that the principles outlined in this book will make a difference between failures and finishers. As I mentioned at the outset, this book is really about management: organizational management, processes management, and financial management. Organizational management brings together various resources for producing and delivering products and services to satisfied customers. Processes management moves materials and services through the organization for producing and delivering products and services to satisfied customers. Financial management funds organization and its processes and oversees created value.

Much of this book consists of theory, tips, and advice learned over a multitude of careers that have refined the planning process to what it is today. Budgeting has come to fruition through hundreds of thousands of careers. More careers give it greater refinement. The budget activity described in this book is relatively brief compared to the total activity that entrepreneurs spend for making their companies successful. Most of the activity occurs during the course of the fiscal year to which the last two chapters are devoted. This is the most important timeframe for the budget process.

I bring up the priority of management, because the key to finishing well is management. Budgeting is really about the entire scope of business and financial management. The budget is not an isolated activity that companies must squeeze into its already busy schedule. While it is not the sum of management, it is an essential component for business management.

As that component, it guides management in unlocking the door to solutions for the challenges confronting the company. Successful management begins with thinking through the various processes that lead into building and sustaining a business. Successful business management also depends on those who champion sound business practices among which are budgeting and sound internal management controls. The singular takeaway of this book is that all the components of management need addressing for business success. This book focuses on one of the major management components. Management by exception does not refer to "except for." Management is oversight of the business through best practices that lay the foundations for accomplishment and achievement.

From McKinsey to McDonald's, businesses that have exercised the discipline of employing well-tested and proven practices reaped their rewards. Budgeting is one of those well-tested practices. It takes discipline and the recognition that budgeting is not simply a practice undertaken once a year but one that the business integrates as a standard routine. It is not one of those "here we go again" drudgeries that casts a dreary shadow over entrepreneurship. Rather, budgeting is one of the pillars of management that gives guidance and measures the company's vision and strategy. It also lends strength to the business by drawing upon already existing tools and strategies that capitalizes on them for bringing the company to satisfactorily reach its goals. Nothing can be more satisfying to an entrepreneur than the inward voice that says, "Well done."

Endorsements

Written from the C-level, business owner, and investor perspective, *Customer-driven Budgeting* quickly expanded my understanding of the budgeting process, especially as it relates to goals that our business is seeking to achieve through expansion into a new customer segment. As a director of a quickly growing and newly formed business development department, I am responsible for expanding our business outside of our traditional B2B market and opening up new markets that target consumer needs with differentiated products distributed through partnerships, a B2B2C strategy. Not only did Floyd Talbot's book provide me with a strategic perspective and even the vocabulary that was essential to formulating my proposals to our senior leadership team, CFO, and CEO but it also provided me with eminently practical tools to formulate those proposals. The Action Steps at the end of each chapter continue to provide value when my team and I are seeking paths to simply getting things done. This mixture of the strategic and the practical have led to increasing our understanding of how to allocate resources from the perspective of the new customer segments we are targeting and honing our capability to execute, which is the primary metric by which our performance is judged.

—Christian Mackey,
director of Business Development at CPP, Inc.,
the developer of the Myers-Briggs personality testing products

This books offers a framework of critical issues to consider when developing a budget and managing a business. The author has developed a superb step-by-step program that will help both beginners and advance professionals to make informed and well thought out decisions for insuring business success.

—Sergio Retamal
President & CEO
Global4PL Supply Chain Management

I believe that this book will help people better understand all that is involved in the complex area of business finance—particularly in the area of business planning and budgeting. All too often the entrepreneur lacks a real financial background or experience. This book can greatly help make up for that fact and get a given business moving forward successfully.

—Ed Correia
President & CEO
Sagacent Technologies, Inc.

Floyd Talbot's book provides an in-depth system for developing a successful customer-driven budget. He carefully explains how a budget is more than just a set of projected numbers on a financial statement. It is a process that encompasses every aspect of a business's organizational structure and develops critical control points and planning from sales and marketing to production, staffing, and finance. As a CPA, I can attest that it is a must read for any company serious about taking its business to the next level of success.

—Timothy J. Frame, CPA

Notes

Read First!

1. Drucker (2004), p. 64.
2. Cunningham and Fiume (2003).

Chapter 1

1. Hope and Fraser (2003, February).
2. Ibid. 3
3. Jenson. (2001, November), p. 96.
4. Frame, Tim, e-mail letter to author (2012, July 31). Walton and Frame Certified Public Accountants, Sacramento, CA.
5. Avent, Jean Creech, "The Customer Relationship Index: An Overview." OrgPR, LLC (n.d.): 2–4, accessed January 18, 2012, http://bit.ly/9WQN6I

Chapter 2

1. Drucker (2004), p. 117.

Chapter 4

1. Nevin (2002), p. 65.
2. Stuart (2001, March 1).
3. Winton (2002, October 1).
4. Ibid.
5. Robertson (2003, February), pp. 1–9.
6. Alhashmi, Siddiqi, and Akhgar (2005, February 21).
7. Gupta and McDaniel (2002, October).
8. Stevens (2007, June 20).
9. Ibid., 88.
10. Ibid.
11. Ibid., 107.
12. Ibid., 117.
13. Ibid., 125.
14. Ibid., 127.

15. Brown (1996), p. 85.
16. Ibid., 41.

Chapter 5

1. Hightower (2009).
2. Ibid.
3. Deloitte LLP (2011, June), p. 2.
4. Hightower, Kindle location 997.
5. Constituents include customers, vendors, employees, investors, and financial institutions. The individual company business model and industry also dictate financial management application qualification and selection. Financial management applications include the accounting system of record and any ancillary supporting applications for it, such as inventory management, fixed asset management, customer relationship management, and payroll management. These applications may or may not integrate with the accounting software. It is preferred that they do integrate. However, if they do not integrate, it is important to have a control system in place for reconciling such applications.
6. Consult Ron Person's publication *Balanced Scorecards & Operational Dashboards with Microsoft Excel* (Wiley Publishing, Inc.) for methods of developing a step-by-step guide for creating operational dashboards for measuring and reporting on business performance. This would be a great supplement for your budget process.
7. Beasley, Branson, and Hancock (2010).
8. Ibid., 3.
9. Deloitte, p. 3.

Chapter 6

1. For more information on developing KPI metrics, consult the following websites: (1) The KPI Library (http://bit.ly/3j4OzG) provides KPI dashboards for various financial accounting software applications. It requires a sign up for access to certain KPI information. (2) RapidBI.com (http://bit.ly/AfwV1D) introduces KPIs and a number of useful indicators for various business segments. (3) SmartKPIs.com (http://bit.ly/LAQ07d) identifies over 1,100 KPIs to choose from, for measuring business performance for your company.
2. Person (2009), pp. 107–133.
3. BWise Business in Control (2011, November 11).

4. Hightower, Kindle location 393.
5. Deloitte Development, LLC (2010, February), p. 14.

Chapter 7

1. Hightower, Location 579.
2. Drucker (2004), p. 18.
3. Siegel, Shim and Hartman (1992), p. 250.
4. Drucker (2004), p. 5.

Chapter 8

1. Armstrong (1999), pp. 278–290.

Chapter 9

1. Sagacent Technologies, Inc., http://www.sagacent.com/solutions/profes-sional-services.html, accessed April 10, 2012.
2. For other evaluation techniques, consult Siegel et al., *The McGraw-Hill Pocket Guide: 201 Decision-Making Tools for Managers* (1992).

Chapter 12

1. Bechet, Thomas P., "Developing Staffing Strategies that Work: Implement-ing Pragmatic Non-traditional Approaches," *The Walker Group* (accessed July 24, 2012), http://www.nardoni.com/BechetStaffingArticle.pdf, 1.
2. Ibid., 3–13.
3. Ibid.; Frame (2012)

Chapter 14

1. Brown (1996), p. 50.
2. Ibid., 51.
3. Ibid., 57.
4. Accenture "Achieving High Performance: the Value of Benchmarking." CFO.com (accessed March 17, 2012), http://bit.ly/FOIweG, 2–3. Registra-tion required for access.
5. Ibid.
6. The RMA, http://bit.ly/xzu7th, accessed March 20, 2012. There are a num-ber of free publications you can download in PDF format to aid you in the

interpretation of financial statements. One such highly useful publication is the *Annual Statements Studies: Financial Ratio Benchmarks, 2011–2012*. This publication identifies a list of industries and gives detailed information on the use and interpretation of specific types of financial ratios.

7. Siegel et al. (1992).

Chapter 15

1. Kaplan and Norton (2001), pp. 280–295.
2. Chang (2012, July 2).
3. Berry (2012).
4. Anderson (2004, September 7).
5. Myers (2001, December).
6. Parmenter (extract from "Pareto's 80/20 Rule for the Corporate Accountant" published by John Wiley & Sons), Waymark Solutions Limited, http://davidparmenter.com/files/how-to-implement-quarterly-rolling-planning.pdf, accessed July 17, 2012, pp. 2–3.
7. Bragg (2010, June 13).

Appendix B

1. Harmon, Hensel, and Lukes (2006, February 15), pp. 1–4.
2. Ibid.
3. Ibid.
4. Ibid., 3.

Appendix C

1. Frazzetto (2010, March 10).
2. Ibid.
3. Davison (2003, December 9).
4. Poe (2010, August).
5. Taylor (2009, March), p. 5.
6. Ibid., 13.
7. Borowski (2012, January 17).
8. Internal Revenue Service.

Bibliography

Accenture. (2011). *Achieving High Performance: the Value of Benchmarking.* CFO: Business Intelligence Center. http://bit.ly/FOIweG (accessed March 17, 2012).

Advent Design Corporation. (2012). *Plan-Design-Automate-Produce.* http://bit.ly/LNwRmn (accessed May 23, 2012).

Alhashmi, S. M., Siddiqi, J., & Akhgar B. (2005). *Knowledge Management for Business Performance Improvement.* Social Science Research Network. February 21, 2005. http://bit.ly/KNgqAW (accessed June 15, 2012).

Anderson, D. J. (2004). *Drucker on Adaptive vs. Plan-driven.* David J. Anderson and Associates. September 7, 2004. http://agilemanagement.net/index.php/site/comments/drucker_on_adaptive_vs._plan-driven (accessed July 11, 2012).

Armstrong, J. S. (1999). Sales forecasting. In M. J. Baker (Ed.), *IEBM Encyclopedia of Marketing; 2nd Edition* (pp. 278–290). London: International Thompson Business Press.

Avent, J. C. (2012). *OrgPR, LLC.* http://bit.ly/9WQN6I (accessed January 18, 2012).

Beasley, M. S., Branson, B. C., & Hancock, B. V. (2010). *Developing Key Risk Indicators to Strengthen Enterprise Risk Management: How Key Risk Indicators can Sharpen Focus on Emerging Risks.* Committee of Sponsoring Organizations of the Treadway Commission (COSO), www.coso.org. December 2010. http://bit.ly/GXRF30 (accessed March 3, 2012).

Bechet, T. P. (2012). *The Walker Group.* Nardoni Strategic Solutions. 2012. http://www.nardoni.com/BechetStaffingArticle.pdf (accessed July 24, 2012).

Berry, T. (2012). *5 Points on Business Planning and Imminent Change.* AllBusiness. http://www.allbusiness.com/company-activities-management/management-change-management/11790833-1.html#axzz20M0WpdmT (accessed July 11, 2012).

Borowski, D. (2012). *2012 Outsourcing Checklist.* Business Finance: Best Practices for Finance Executives. January 17, 2012. http://bit.ly/yQKqfN (accessed January 19, 2012).

Bragg, S. M. (2012). *Cost Accounting Fundamentals: Essential Concepts and Examples.* Centennial, CO: Steven M. Bragg.

Bragg, S. M. (2012). *The Accounting Procedures Guidebook.* Centennial, CO: Accounting Tools, LLC.

Bragg, S. M. (2011). *Wiley GAAP 2012: Interpretation and Application of Generally Accepted Accounting Principles.* USA: Wiley.

Bragg, S. M. (2010). *Should I Use a Rolling Forecast?* Accounting Tools. June 13, 2010. http://www.accountingtools.com/questions-and-answers/should-i-use-a-rolling-forecast.html (accessed July 17, 2012).

Brown, M. G. (1996). *Keeping Score: Using the Right Metrics to Drive World-class Performance.* New York: Productivity, Inc.

Brydges, B. (2012). *Business Finance: Best Practices for Finance Executives.* January 10, 2012. http://bit.ly/A3ES8r (accessed March 10, 2012).

BWise Business in Control in CFO Business Intelligence Center. (2011). *Four Steps to Incorporate Risk Management into Your Organization.* November 21, 2011. http://bit.ly/KVLRzz (accessed March 13, 2012).

Chang, A. (2012). *Nokia's Contingency Plan: 5 Possible Company-saving Scenarios.* Wired Magazine. July 2, 2012. http://www.wired.com/gadgetlab/2012/07/nokia-says-it-has-backup-plan (accessed July 11, 2012).

Cunningham, J. E. & Fiume, O. J. (2003). *Real Number: Management Accounting in the Lean Organization.* Durham, NC: Managing Time Press.

Customer Services Benchmarking Association. (2012). *The Benchmarking Network.* http://bit.ly/MJkNSk (accessed February 2, 2012).

Dale C. (2012). *About Us.* http://bit.ly/wHIWRP (accessed April 3, 2012).

Davison, D. (2012). *Top 10 Risks of Offshore Outsourcing.* ZDNet. December 9, 2003. http://www.zdnet.com/news/top-10-risks-of-offshore-outsourcing/299274 (accessed July 26, 2012).

Delloite LLP. (2011). *Evaluating the Tone at the Top: Practical Suggestions for Audit Committees.* Delloite: Center for Corporate Governance United States. June 2011. (accessed February 3, 2012).

Deloitte Development, LLP. (2010). *Strategies for Going Public* (3rd ed.). Deloitte. February 2010. http://bit.ly/L8QTbf (accessed March 16, 2012).

Drucker, P. F. (2004). *The Daily Drucker.* New York: HarperCollins.

Epstein, B. J., Nach, R., & Bragg, S. (2007). *Wiley GAAP 2008: Interpretation and Application of Generally Accepted Accounting Principles.* Hoboken, NJ: John Wiley & Sons.

Feldt, R., Brown, R., & Parshay, K. (2008). *Integrating Process Improvements and Internal Controsl.* Lean Accounting News. December 2008. http://bit.ly/L07eOb (accessed June 9, 2012).

Frame, T. (2012) E-mail letter to author, July 31, 2012, Walton and Frame Certified Public Accountants, Sacramento, CA.

Frazzetto, A. (2010). *10 Steps for Multi-sourcing Success.* March 10, 2010. http://bit.ly/ctlmp0 (accessed February 10, 2012).

Gaebler V. (2012). *Gaebler Ventures.* January 11, 2011. http://bit.ly/KCCjD5 (accessed January 25, 2012).

Gupta, A. & McDaniel, J. (2002). Creating competitive advantage by effectively manageing knowledge: A framework for knowledge management. *Journal of Knowledge Management Practice.* October 2002. http://bit.ly/Ls2ihO (accessed June 15, 2012).

Harmon, E., Hensel, S., & Lukes, T. (2006). Meauring performance in services. *The McKinsey Quarterly.* February 2006. http://bit.ly/LWYMg5 (accessed April 23, 2012).

Hightower, R. (2009). *Internal Controls Policies and Procedures, Kindle Edition.* Hoboken, NJ: John Wiley & Sons.

Hope, J. & Fraser, R. (2003, February). Who needs budgets. *Harvard Business Review,* 1–8.

Internal Revenue Service. (2011). *Independent Contractor (Self-employed) or Employee.* October 2011. http://1.usa.gov/DLM9O (accessed June 1, 2012).

Internet Center for Management and Business Administration, Inc. (2012). *Market Definition.* http://bit.ly/3YiAch (accessed April 3, 2012).

Jenson, M. C. (2001, November) Corporate Budeting is Broken—Let's Fix It. *Harvard Business Review,* 94–101.

Kaplan, R. S. & Norton, D. P. (2001). *The Strategy-focused Organization: How Balanced Scorecard Companies Thrive in the New Business Environment.* Boston, MA: Harvard Business Review.

Kawasaki, G. (2011). http://bit.ly/8WneF3 (accessed December 27, 2011).

Kawasaki, G. (2011). *Presentation Magazine.* http://bit.ly/8WneF3 (accessed December 27, 2011).

Lambert, S. J., Chen, K. H., & Lambert, J. C. (1996). Overhead Cost Pools. *Internal Auditor in CBC Interactive Business Network Resource Library.* October 1996. http://bit.ly/GXY4yY (accessed March 24, 2012).

Messick, R. (1998). Benchmarking Your Insurance Coverage. *The Free Library (Journal of Property Management).* March 1, 1998. http://bit.ly/M1ms53 (accessed March 7, 2012).

Myers, R. (2001). Budgets on a roll. *Journal of Accountancy.* December 2001. http://www.journalofaccountancy.com/Issues/2001/Dec/BudgetsOnARoll.htm (accessed July 17, 2012).

Nevin, P. (2002). *Balanced Scorecard Step-by-Step: Maximizing Peformance and Maintaining Rsults.* New York: John Wiley & Sons.

OPEX Resources. (2011). *OPEX Resources.* http://bit.ly/upwVs6 (accessed December 27, 2011).

Parmenter, D. (2012). *How to Implement Quarterly Roling Planning - and Get it Right the First Time (extract from Pareto's 80/20 Rule for the Corporate Accountant published by John Wiley & Sons, Inc.). Waymark Solutions Limited.* http://davidparmenter.com/files/how-to-implement-quarterly-rolling-planning.pdf (accessed July 17, 2012).

Perry, S. C. (2001). The Relationship Between Written Business Plans and the Failure of Small Business in the U.S. *Allbusiness.com.* July 1, 2001. http://bit.ly/wgOa2L (accessed March 16, 2012).

Person, R. (2009). *Balanced Scorecards & Operational Dashboards with Microsoft Excel.* Indianapolis: Wiley Publishing, Inc.

Poe, W. (2000). Import/Export Challenges: International Trade Must Overcome Legal, Tax, and Otehr Obstacles. *STL Commerce Magazine.* August 2000. http://bit.ly/A4paxQ (accessed March 6, 2012).

RapidBI. (2012). *Business & Organizational Development Tools, Training & Services—Human Resources, OD, and Leadership.* http://bit.ly/AfwV1D (accessed June 3, 2012).

Robertson, J. (2003). Metrics for KM and CM. *Step Two Designs.* February 2003. http://www.steptwo.com.au/files/kmc_metrics.pdf (accessed June 16, 2012).

Sagacent Technologies, Inc. (2012). *Solutions Technology Services, Managed Services, Strategic Technology Consulting.* http://bit.ly/MG8TFi (accessed April 3, 2012).

Siegel, J. G., Shim, J. K., & Hartman, S. W. (1992) *The McGraw-Hill Pocket Guide to Business Finance: 201 Decision-Making Tools for Managers.* New York: McGraw-Hill, Inc..

SmartKPIs.com. (2012). *1100 Key Performance Indicators (KPI) Examples on smartKPIs.com.* http://bit.ly/LAQ07d (accessed June 10, 2012).

Stevens, M. (2007). *Isn't it Time for Financial Management Training for Your Staff?* June 20, 2007. http://bit.ly/Krslek (accessed February 10, 2012).

Stuart, A. (2001). Fighting Information Overload. *CFO Magazine.* March 1, 2001. http://www.cfo.com/article.cfm/3002204?f=search (accessed June 15, 2012).

Taylor, J. (2009). Next Generation Warranty Systems. *Decision Management Systems.* March 2009. http://bit.ly/yPtF28 (accessed May 15, 2012).

The KPI Library. (2012). *The KPI Library.* http://bit.ly/3j4OzG (accessed June 5, 2012).

The Risk Management Association. (2012). *eStatement Studies.* http://bit.ly/xzu7th (accessed March 20, 2012).

Wal-Mart Corporate. (2011). *Wal-Mart Corporate.* http://bit.ly/EtLJA (accessed December 27, 2011).

Winton, K. (2002). Knowledge Management: An Unnatural Act? *CFO Magazine.* October 1, 2002. http://www.cfo.com/article.cfm/3006922/2/c_2984382?f=search (accessed June 15, 2012).

Index

OTHER TITLES IN MANAGERIAL ACCOUNTING COLLECTION

Kenneth A. Merchant, Editor

- *The Small Business Controller* by Richard O. Hanson
- *Sustainability Reporting: Managing for Wealth and Corporate Health* by Gwendolen White
- *Business Planning and Entrepreneurship: An Accounting Approach* by Michael Kraten
- *Corporate Investment Decisions: Principles and Practice* by Michael Pogue
- *Revenue Management A Path to Increased Profits* by Ronald Huefner
- *Cost Management and Control in Government Fighting the Cost War Through Leadership Driven Management* by Dale Geiger
- *Drivers of Successful Controllership: Activities, People, and Connecting with Management* by Jurgen Weber
- *Setting Performance Targets* by Carolyn Stringer
- *Strategic Cost Analysis* by Roger Hussey

Announcing the Business Expert Press Digital Library

Concise E-books Business Students Need for Classroom and Research

This book can also be purchased in an e-book collection by your library as
- a one-time purchase,
- that is owned forever,
- allows for simultaneous readers,
- has no restrictions on printing, and
- can be downloaded as PDFs from within the library community.

Our digital library collections are a great solution to beat the rising cost of textbooks. e-books can be loaded into their course management systems or onto student's e-book readers.

The **Business Expert Press** digital libraries are very affordable, with no obligation to buy in future years. For more information, please visit **www.businessexpertpress.com/librarians**. To set up a trial in the United States, please contact **Adam Chesler** at *adam.chesler@businessexpertpress .com* for all other regions, contact **Nicole Lee** at *nicole.lee@igroupnet.com*.